COGNITIVE BEHAVIORAL THERAPY

Retrain Your Brain, Improve Self-Esteem and Self-Discipline, Learn Emotional Intelligence and Change Your Life

Nicole Gladwell

© Copyright 2020 by Nicole Gladwell. All right reserved.

The work contained herein has been produced with the intent to provide relevant knowledge and information on the topic on the topic described in the title for entertainment purposes only. While the author has gone to every extent to furnish up to date and true information, no claims can be made as to its accuracy or validity as the author has made no claims to be an expert on this topic. Notwithstanding, the reader is asked to do their own research and consult any subject matter experts they deem necessary to ensure the quality and accuracy of the material presented herein.

This statement is legally binding as deemed by the Committee of Publishers Association and the American Bar Association for the territory of the United States. Other jurisdictions may apply their own legal statutes. Any reproduction, transmission, or copying of this material contained in this work without the express written consent of the copyright holder shall be deemed as a copyright violation as per the current legislation in force on the date of publishing and the subsequent time thereafter. All additional works derived from this material may be claimed by the holder of this copyright.

The data, depictions, events, descriptions, and all other information forthwith are considered to be true, fair, and accurate unless the work is expressly described as a work of fiction. Regardless of the nature of this work, the Publisher is exempt from any responsibility of actions taken by the reader in conjunction with this work. The Publisher acknowledges that the reader acts of their own accord and releases the author and Publisher of any responsibility for the observance of tips, advice, counsel, strategies, and techniques that may be offered in this volume.

TABLE OF CONTENTS

Introduction 1
Chapter 1 *What Is Cognitive Behavioral Therapy?* 2
Chapter 2 *When Is Cognitive Behavioral Therapy Used?* 9
Chapter 3 *What Can Cognitive Behavioral Therapy Treat?* 20
Chapter 4 *Cbt And Unhelpful Thinking Styles* 47
Chapter 5 *Examples Of Cbt* 52
Chapter 6 *Preventing Relapses With Cbt* 66
Conclusion 73
Description 75

INTRODUCTION

Cognitive Behavioral Therapy has been an increasingly hot topic in psychology in the past few years. More and more therapists and psychiatrists adapt to this type of speaking therapy due to its proven effectiveness in treating common mental disorders like anxiety and depression. In this book, you will learn about CBT in great depth, including the following topics in particular;

What You Will Learn in This Book

This book will explore the theories and functions of Cognitive Behavioral Therapy and how it works to treat disorders like Anxiety and Depression. We will start this book by learning more about how CBT works when used and how it compares to other therapy types. We will then learn about what anxiety is, its symptoms, and different styles. We will then learn about depression, the science behind it, the different types, and its symptoms. By this point in the book, you should have a strong understanding of how anxiety and depression work and how CBT can effectively treat symptoms. Towards this book's center, we will be looking at the benefits and drawbacks of choosing CBT as your treatment method. This chapter is essential in determining if CBT is the right treatment method for the disorder you are looking to treat. After that, we will focus on using CBT to specifically manage a person's anxiety/depression and use other methods to manage these disorders. We will take a look into mindfulness, meditation, lifestyle changes, and practicing gratitude.

Who This Book Is for

Are you someone that feels like their mental disorders always burden them? Do you feel like something is holding you back from reaching your full potential? Are you feeling stuck and are struggling to get out of this slump? If you identify with this, this book can help you learn Cognitive Behavioral Therapy to treat your disorders. Still, it will also equip you with the right knowledge to understand what is happening and why. It is crucial to learn as much as you can regarding your mental health, and from there, apply the CBT methods you will learn to treat your situation correctly.

Overall, I wrote this book to teach you how to use CBT and educate you on all topics related to understanding why CBT uses its strategy. Understanding that, people are more likely to stay committed to the process than give up if they don't see results right away. Without further ado, let's dive into this book.

CHAPTER 1
What Is Cognitive Behavioral Therapy?

Cognitive Behavioral Therapy has been an increasingly hot topic in psychology in the past few years. More and more therapists and psychiatrists adapt to this type of speaking therapy due to its proven effectiveness in treating common mental disorders like anxiety and depression. Although we hear about this term a lot, what exactly is it? This chapter will look at what Cognitive Behavioral Therapy is and when you can use it.

What Is Cognitive Behavioral Therapy (CBT)?

So, what exactly is it? The foundation of Cognitive Behavioral Therapy is the theory that a person's thoughts (cognition), emotion, and behavior are all constantly interacting with one another; therefore, if one of these three components are affected, the rest will be affected as well. CBT is an umbrella term for many different therapies that share standard details.

The three components that Cognitive Behavioral Therapy (CBT) focuses on are the following;

CognitionResponsible for how we think and what we think.
- Emotion

Based on how we feel.
- Behavior

Based on how we act.

These three components all support the theory that if a person merely changes their thoughts or the way they think, it will impact their feelings, ultimately determining their behavior.

In simple terms, this means that people who may be having negative or unrealistic thoughts that cause them distress could result in behavioral problems. When a person is suffering from psychological pain, they perceive certain situations that can become contorted, causing negative behaviors.

How Does CBT Work?

Cognitive Behavioral Therapy works by emphasizing the relationship between our thoughts, feelings, and behaviors. When you begin to change any of these components, you start to initiate change in the others. CBT aims to help lower the amount you worry and increase the overall quality of your life.

Here are the eight basic principles of how Cognitive Behavioral Therapy works:

1. CBT will help provide a new perspective of understanding your problems.

Often, when an individual has been living with a problem for a long time in their life, they may have developed unique ways of understanding it and dealing with it. Usually, this just maintains the problem or makes it worse. CBT is useful in helping you look at your situation from a new perspective, and this will help you learn other ways of understanding your problem and learning a new way of dealing with it.

2. CBT will help you generate new skills to work out your problem. You probably know that understanding a problem is one matter, and dealing with it is entirely another can of worms. To help start changing your situation, you will need to develop new skills to transform your thoughts, behaviors, and emotions that affect your anxiety and mental health. For instance, CBT will help you achieve new ideas about your problem and begin to use and test them in your daily life. Therefore, you will be more capable of making up your mind regarding the root issue causing these negative symptoms.

3. CBT relies on teamwork and collaboration between the client and therapist (or program).

CBT will require you to be actively involved in the entire process, and your thoughts and ideas are extremely valuable right from the beginning of the therapy. You are the expert when it comes to your thoughts and problems. The therapist is the expert when it comes to acknowledging the emotional issues. By working as a team, you will identify your problems and have your therapist better address them. Historically, the more the therapy advances, the more the client finds techniques to deal with the symptoms.

4. The goal of CBT is to help the client become their therapist.

Therapy is expensive; we all know that. One of CBT's goals is not to have you become overly dependent on your therapist because it is not feasible to have therapy forever. When treatment comes to an end, and you do not become your therapist, you will be at high risk for a relapse. However, if you can become your therapist, you will be in a good spot to face the hurdles that life throws at you. Also, scientists proved that having confidence in your ability to face hardship is one of the best predictors of maintaining the valuable information you got from therapy. By playing an active role during your sessions, you will gain the confidence needed to face your problems when the sessions are over.

5. CBT is brief and time-limited.

As a rule of thumb, CBT therapy sessions typically last from 10 to 20 sessions. Statistically, when therapy goes on for many months, there is a higher risk of the client becoming dependent on the therapist. Once you have gained a new perspective and understanding of your problem and have equipped yourself with the right skills, you can solve future problems. It is crucial in CBT for you to try out your new skills in the real world. By actually dealing with your own problem hands-on without the security of recurring therapy sessions, you will be able to build confidence in your ability to become your therapist.

6. CBT is direction based and structured.

CBT typically relies on a fundamental strategy called 'guided recovery.' By setting up some experiments with your therapist, you will be able to experiment with new ideas to see if they reflect your reality accurately. In other words, your therapist is your guide while you are making discoveries in CBT. The therapist will not tell you whether you are right or wrong, but instead, they will help develop ideas and experiments to test these ideas.

7. CBT is based on the present, "here and now."

Although we know that our childhood and developmental history play a significant role in who we are today, one of CBT's principles is looking at the relationship between what caused the problem and what maintains the problem presently. In many cases, the reasons that maintain a problem are different from those that initially caused it. For example, if you fall off while riding a horse, you may become afraid of horses. Your fear will continue to be maintained if you begin avoiding all horses and refusing to ride one again. In this example, the fall caused anxiety, but you continue to maintain it by avoiding fear. Unfortunately, you cannot change the fact that you had fallen off the horse, but you can change your behaviors when it comes to avoidance. CBT primarily focuses on the factors that are maintaining the problem because these factors are susceptible to change.

8. Worksheet exercises are significant elements of CBT therapy.

Unfortunately, reading about CBT or going to one therapy session a week is not enough to change our ingrained patterns of thinking and behaving. During CBT, the client is always encouraged to apply their new skills into their daily lives. Although most people find CBT therapy sessions very intriguing, it does not lead to change in reality if you do not exercise the skills you have learned.

These eight principles will be your guiding light throughout your Cognitive Behavioral Therapy. By learning, understanding, and applying these eight principles, you will be in an excellent position to invest your time and energy into becoming your therapist and start reaching your goals. Based on research, individuals who are highly motivated to try exercises outside of sessions tend to find more value in therapy than those who don't. Keep in mind that other external factors still affect your success, but your motivation is one of the most significant factors. By following CBT using the principles above, you should be able to remain highly motivated throughout CBT.

The History of CBT

Albert Ellis and Aaron T. Beck developed the earliest forms of cognitive-behavioral therapy in the mid-90s. At the time, it was called Rational

Emotive Behavior Therapy (REBT). REBT is a type of cognitive therapy that focuses on fixing emotional and behavioral problems. The main goal of REBT is to shift irrational beliefs to rational ones. Rational Emotive Behavior Therapy encourages an individual to figure out their irrational personal beliefs and then influence them to challenge those beliefs by testing them in reality.

Albert Ellis proposed that every single person carries a unique set of assumptions regarding ourselves and our world. He suggested that we use that set of beliefs to serve and guide us through life and has a significant influence on our reactions to different situations that we experience. However, some people's set of assumptions are irrational, leading to them acting and reacting in inappropriate ways and can even inhibit your success. This term is called 'basic irrational assumptions.'

An example of an irrational assumption will be if an individual assumes they are a failure because everyone they know doesn't express love for them. This assumption leads them to be seeking out approval and feeling rejected constantly. Since this individual sees all actions and interactions from the lens of this assumption, they will feel dissatisfied if they did not receive enough compliments. According to Albert Ellis, these are other popular and common irrational assumptions:

- The idea that you should be competent at everything you do
- The idea that when things are not the way you want them to be it is catastrophic
- The idea that you cannot control your happiness
- The idea that you need to be dependent on somebody stronger than you
- The idea that your history heavily influences your present life
- The idea that it will be a disaster if you don't find the perfect solution to human problems

Aaron Beck has a similar therapy system to Albert Ellis's, but his version is more common for treating depression than anxiety. Therapists typically use this therapy system to help the client notice the negative thoughts and logic errors that lead them to be depressed. They also use this system to challenge an individual's dysfunctional thoughts, try to interpret situations differently, and apply a different perspective of thinking into their everyday lives.

Typically, if a person has many negative automatic thoughts, it is likely that they would become depressed. These thoughts will continue even though there is conflicting evidence. Aaron Beck identified three mechanisms in the mid-90s that he thought caused depression:

- The cognitive triad (automatic negative thinking)
- Negative self-schemas
- Errors in logic (inaccurate information processing)

Aaron Beck posited that "the cognitive triad" includes three harmful thinking types that individuals suffer from depression showcase. It consisted of negative thoughts about yourself, the world, and the future.

These types of thoughts tend to appear automatically in depressed people and are quite spontaneous. As these three types of thoughts begin to interact, they interfere with our brain's normal cognitive functions and lead to perception impairment, memory impairment, and difficulty with problem-solving. The person will likely become obsessed with these negative thoughts.

Aaron Beck identified numerous illogical thinking processes in his study of cognitive distortions. He concluded that these irrational thought patterns are self-deprecating and cause many anxieties and depression symptoms. Here are a few of his irrational thinking processes:

- Arbitrary interference: This thinking process involves concluding with insufficient and irrelevant evidence. For instance, thinking and feeling worthless because of the theme park you were going to have closed due to weather.
- Selective Abstraction: This thinking process involves focusing on one aspect of a circumstance and ignoring all other elements. For example, you feel responsible for your team losing a volleyball match even though you are just one team member.
- Magnification: The thinking process involves the exaggeration of importance during a negative situation. For example, if you accidentally scratched your car, you see yourself as a terrible driver.
- Minimization: This thinking process involves underplaying the importance of an event. For instance, you get praised by your boss for your excellent work, but you see this is a trivial matter.
- Overgeneralization: This thinking process involves drawing negative conclusions due to one single event. For example, you usually get straight As in university, but you failed one exam, and therefore, you think you are stupid.
- Personalization: This thinking process involves associating the negative feelings of other people with yourself. For example, your boss looked angry when she entered the office today; therefore, she must be angry with you.

Aaron Beck and Albert Ellis have developed many theories and structured behaviors that led to the modern-day development of Cognitive Behavioral Therapy. Due to their research in the mid-90s, studies have concluded that 80% of adults benefit from Cognitive Behavioral Therapy. This result is a massive success in therapy, as many people prefer talking therapy over medical treatment to help mental disorders like anxiety and depression.

CBT Today

In today's society, Cognitive Behavioral Therapy is used to treat mental disorders, primarily anxiety and depression. We will look at these treatments in more detail in further chapters of this book.

Due to its long history and development, CBT is a practical and time-saving form of psychotherapy. CBT focuses on your here-and-now problems that come up in daily life. It helps people make sense of their surroundings and events that happen around them. CBT is very structured, time-saving, and problem-focused. These advantages are why CBT is one of the most popular techniques for dealing with mental disorders in our fast-paced modern lives.

In the present day, CBT works by helping clients recognize, question, and change the thoughts that relate to the emotional and behavioral reactions that cause them difficulty. Using CBT to monitor and record thoughts during undesirable situations, people begin to learn that the way they think contributes to their emotional problems. Modern-day Cognitive Behavioral Therapy helps reduce emotional problems by teaching individuals to:

- Identify any distortions in their thinking process
- See their thoughts as ideas rather than facts
- Take a step back from their thoughts to look at situations from another perspective

The new CBT model used in the present day focuses on the relationship between thoughts and behaviors. Both can influence each other. There are three levels and types of thoughts:

- Conscious thoughts: These are rational thoughts that people think with complete awareness
- Automatic thoughts: These are the thoughts that move very quickly; you are likely not to be fully aware of their movement. For this reason, it is difficult to check them for accuracy. A person suffering from mental health problems may have thoughts that are entirely not logical.
- Schemas: These are the core beliefs and personal values when it comes to processing information. Our childhood and other life experiences shape our Schemas.

The modern-day CBT is slightly different from the previous type, which was mainly REBT. The CBT we use now is used to treat a plethora of mental disorders, whereas we used REBT in the past, mostly to treat depression and anxiety. Moreover, depression and anxiety were not as prevalent in the mid-90s compared to its presence now. In the later chapters, we will discuss why mental orders like depression and anxiety are more common in today's society.

Who Uses CBT?

Many people use Cognitive Behavioral Therapy, whether it is to help others or solve their problems. The most general answer to who uses CBT would be a therapist and somebody with a mental disorder. However, CBT professionals use it within the psychology space, alcohol addiction, substance abuse, eating disorders, phobias, and anger management. CBT is a flexible tool that many types of people can use to treat the problem at hand.

CBT can benefit you even if you are not facing a severe problem like mentioned above. Many people who used to go to therapy continue to use CBT to maintain a healthy mindset. CBT has also proved useful for events like interventions. However, the people that typically use and gain the most from CBT are the people who are willing to spend the time and energy analyzing their thoughts and feelings. Since self-analysis generally is difficult, many people may give up after realizing how uncomfortable it could be. However, CBT is very well-suited for the people looking for short term treatment that does not require medication. This strategy is very suitable for people who don't want to take drugs to manage disorders like depression and anxiety.

CHAPTER 2
When Is Cognitive Behavioral Therapy Used?

When Is CBT Used?

Now that you have learned how CBT works in the first chapter of this book, we will look at why CBT is a method of choice for professionals worldwide.

The main answer to this question is that professionals use CBT to pursue therapy to help their clients with their problems. These problems are often disorders such as depression, anxiety, or more serious ones like OCD and PTSD.

The most common uses for CBT are depression and generalized anxiety disorder to dive a little more in-depth. However, CBT is also used and is very useful for other conditions such as:

- Body Dysmorphic Disorder
- Eating Disorders
- Chronic Low Back Pain
- Personality Disorders
- Psychosis
- Schizophrenia
- Substance Used Disorders

Since CBT focuses on the relationship between thoughts, emotions, and behavior, those who suffer from disorders that stem from mental health may find it helpful to try CBT. Most modern-day therapists opt for CBT as the best technique to handle the client's problems as it covers numerous disorders, and the client can learn it and continue to use it without the therapist's help.

On a more straightforward note, professionalism as a method of general therapy. Professionals could choose this when they attend therapy sessions to remain in touch with their thoughts and feelings. Although this person may not be suffering from any particular disorder, CBT is a helpful tool for someone who wants to organize their thoughts.

CBT and Other Methods of Therapy

Cognitive Behavioral Therapy and other types of behavioral therapies share a lot in common and have many significant differences. The typical behavioral therapies that you may see on TV and movies seem to involve a lot of dream interpretation or complex discussion of childhood experiences. This type of therapy is very outdated compared to CBT. Not many therapists in modern-day use this type of treatment. CBT is different from other therapies by focusing mainly on how a person's thoughts, emotions, and behaviors are connected.

Examples of Other Types of Therapy

In this section, we will look at other types of therapy and how they compare to CBT. Although CBT is an effective treatment for anxiety and depression, there are alternate methods to help its effectiveness if we practice them simultaneously. Techniques such as mindfulness and meditation, improving your physical health, preventing bad habits like procrastination, and practicing gratitude go a long way in managing anxiety and depression. Let's take a look at these other methods.

- Psychodynamic or Psychoanalytic Psychotherapy

In psychodynamic (or psychoanalytic psychotherapy), the therapist helps the person open up, speak about their thoughts, and express their feelings. After listening to you open up, the therapist will tell you what they observe, such as patterns or problems in your life or your ways of thinking.

Psychodynamic therapy is similar to psychoanalytic therapy in that it is an in-depth form of talk-therapy based on principles and theories of psychoanalysis. However, psychodynamic therapy is not as focused on the relationship between the client and therapist but focuses on the client's relationship with their external world. Usually, psychodynamic therapy does not last as long as psychoanalytic therapy when it comes to the number of sessions and the frequency of those sessions; however, this differs by case.

Psychodynamic therapy is commonly used to treat depression or anxiety and other severe psychological disorders. It focuses primarily on the people who may have lost meaning in their lives and struggle to maintain and form personal relationships. Studies have found that people who suffer from eating disorders, addiction, and social anxiety disorders benefit from psychodynamic therapy. During psychodynamic therapy, the client is encouraged to speak about anything that comes to mind, including dreams, desires, fantasies, current issues, and the therapist's help. This therapy aims to reduce their depression or anxiety systems and achieve other benefits such as better use of their abilities and talents, increasing self-esteem, and an improved ability to develop and maintain better relationships. The client may continue to experience the benefits even after this therapy has ended. Some patients may find that short-term therapy (less than one year) is sufficient; some other patients may require long-term therapy to gain lasting effects.

Psychodynamic therapy's theories and techniques distinguish it from other forms of therapy. Psychodynamic therapy focuses on acknowledging, recognizing, expressing, understanding, and overcoming contradictory and negative feelings and repressed emotions to improve a person's interpersonal relationships and experiences. Psychodynamic therapy helps the client understand how their previous repressed emotions affect their current behavior, relationships, and decision-making. This type of therapy also aims to help the client who may be aware of their social difficulties but doesn't have the tools or skills to overcome this problem by themselves. During this therapy, the clients will learn to analyze and resolve their current issues and then change their behavior in their existing relationships by using in-depth exploration and analysis of their past experiences and emotions.

- Cognitive Analytical Therapy (CAT)

Cognitive analytical therapy combines CBT and psychodynamic psychotherapy to develop a new hybrid form of therapy. It focuses on your behavior and how this may be causing problems in your life. Then, the therapist presents you with solutions.

- Interpersonal Psychotherapy (IPT)

Interpersonal psychotherapy focuses on a person's relationships and how these could lead to mental illness. This type of therapy includes looking at relationship breakdown, disputing, or other events involving relationships that could cause a person's internal struggles. Then, the therapist will help you to find strategies for dealing with this.

Interpersonal psychotherapy (IPT) is evidence-based, focused, and time-limited approach to treat mental disorders like depression and anxiety. The primary goal of IPT is to improve the quality of a person's social functioning and interpersonal relationships to reduce their distress in those situations. There are four main areas with which IPT helps the client. Firstly, it focuses on addressing interpersonal deficits, such as involvement in unfulfilling relationships and social isolation. Secondly, IPT helps clients manage their unresolved grief, especially if the reason for their distress is related to the loss of a close person in their lives either in the past or recently. Thirdly, IPT can also help with challenging life changes such as moving to another city, divorce, or retirement. Lastly, IPT also helps people dealing with conflict-related relationships such as with co-workers, family members, close friends, or partners.

Scientists initially developed IPT to treat major depressive disorders (MDD). It is also effectively used to treat perinatal depression, eating disorders, drug, and alcohol abuse, dysthymia, and other mood disorders such as bipolar disorder (BPD). IPT is different from traditional therapy types by focusing on the present rather than past relationships or upbringing. This practice is different from CBT because it speaks to maladaptive thoughts and behaviors and how they affect relationships.

The goal of IPT is to change a person's relationship patterns and not their depressive symptoms and target relationship struggles that exacerbate the symptoms. IPT is less structured than CBT as it focuses on the areas that the client has specified without concentrating on their personality traits.

Treatment using IPT usually is in individual therapy sessions and group work that is completed anywhere from 12 weeks to 16 weeks. Its methodology is structured daily and includes assessments throughout the treatment, interviews with the therapist, and homework exercises. The first stage of IPT requires the therapist to assess the client's social history and depressive symptoms within the first three sessions. They examine the client's social history in-depth, noting any changes in the patterns of their relationships. After that, the therapist and client will work as a team to implement the treatment strategies chosen specifically to areas with the most problems. As treatment develops, they may change their targeted problem area. Group sessions are similar to the individual ones because they are semi-structured, focused on interpersonal dynamics, and are time-limited. Group therapies provide clients a safe and supportive environment to practice their interpersonal skills. Pre, mid, and post-treatment sessions also occur in a group therapy format to review the client's individual progress, goals, and strategies.

IPT was developed over 20 years ago and originally intended to be a time-structured treatment for people who had severe depression or anxiety. In recent years, it gained a lot of popularity. IPT practitioners believe that changing a person's social environment is an essential factor in treating depression or anxiety and preventing it. In the beginning, therapists used IPT exclusively for adults, but it has been modified in recent years, so adolescents and older people can benefit.

- Humanistic Therapy

Humanistic therapy is focused on positive psychology and helping a person increase their self-awareness and image of themselves.

- Family and Couple or Systemic Therapies

Family or couples therapy is a kind of group therapy that involves several people who are in close relationships who wish to work through problems together with a therapist's help.

- Mindfulness and Meditation

The most commonly practiced meditation is mindfulness meditation. Mindfulness meditation is a type of mental training practice that focuses your mind on your thoughts and sensations in the present moment. These include; your current emotions, physical feelings, and passing thoughts. Mindfulness meditation usually involves breathing practice, mental imagery, awareness of your mind and body, and muscle and body relaxation. It is typically more accessible for beginners to follow a guided meditation directing them throughout the whole process. It is extremely easy to drift away or fall asleep while in meditation if nobody is guiding you. Once you become more skilled in mindfulness meditation, you can do it without a vocal guide, but this requires strong mental capabilities.

- Medical Treatment

When it comes to anti-depressants, it is the most advertised treatment for depression and anxiety, but it doesn't necessarily mean that it is the most effective. Depression is about chemical imbalances in the brain, but it does not mean that it is only that. Medication can often help relieve moderate to severe depression symptoms, but it does not solve the underlying problem and is not a long-term solution. Like we learned previously, antidepressants come with side effects, and if a person does not wean off properly, they can suffer from withdrawal.

Antidepressants and Anti-anxiety medications are a range of drugs that treat depression, anxiety, and a variety of other mental disorders. They are the most commonly prescribed medications these days. Antidepressants include SSRIs (serotonin reuptake inhibitors), SNRIs (serotonin-norepinephrine reuptake inhibitors, TCAs (tricyclic antidepressants), atypical antidepressants, and MAOIs (monoamine oxidase inhibitors).

Antidepressants and Anti-anxiety medications work by adjusting the brain's neurotransmitters to help correct the balance of chemicals. When a person is in the trenches of torment, depression's pain, and anguish, merely taking a pill can seem like a simple and convenient relief method. However, it is essential to keep in mind that brain chemicals' imbalance isn't the only cause of depression. Instead, it is a combination of that and other psychological, biological, and social factors that include coping skills, relationships, and lifestyle, all of which medication would not address. However, it does not mean the antidepressants are not sufficient. When a person's depression is on a severe level, antidepressants can be lifesaving or very helpful. Although medication can help people relieve some of their symptoms, antidepressants do not cure depression and are not a recommended long-term solution. However, as more time goes by, people who originally had found antidepressants to be useful can fall back into depression. This effect can happen to the people who stop taking the medication. Antidepressants also come with undesirable side effects, so people need to consider the pros and cons of taking depression medication if you are considering it.

Comparisons Between CBT and Other Therapies

Both CBT and other behavioral therapies have common approaches, such as:

- The therapist and client work as a team to understand that the client is the expert on their thoughts while the therapist has theoretical and technical expertise.
- Treatments are often short term (usually lasting between 6 - 20 sessions). The client actively participates in the treatment inside and outside of the sessions. Homework and worksheets are often mandatory.
- The therapist aims to help the client realize that they are strong and capable of choosing to have positive thoughts and behaviors.
- Treatment is aimed to resolve present-day problems and is goal-oriented. The therapy involves achieving goals by working step by step.
- The client and therapist choose their goals for therapy together and track their progress throughout the treatment.

The foundation of CBT is the theory that thoughts influence feelings and that a person's emotional response to a problem comes from how they interpreted the situation. Here's an example to help you further understand: Imagine feeling your heart's sensations beating irregularly fast and feeling shortness of breath. If these symptoms occurred while you were sitting quietly at home, you would likely assume that it is a medical condition like a heart attack, which will cause anxiety and worry. However, if these symptoms occurred while you were running outside, you would likely not attribute it to a medical condition, and therefore it will not lead to anxiety and worry. Do you see here that different interpretations of the same sensations (e.g., heart racing and shortness of breath) can lead to different emotions entirely?

CBT suggests that many of the emotions that we are feeling are entirely due to the thoughts that we are thinking. In other words, our feelings come from how we perceive and interpret our environment or a situation. Sometimes these ideas and thoughts become distorted or biased. For example, an individual may interpret an ambiguous text message as personal rejection when they may not have any evidence to support that. Other individuals may begin to set unrealistic expectations for themselves regarding being accepted by others. These thoughts contribute to illogical, biased, or distorted thinking processes, which then affect our emotions. In CBT, clients will learn to distinguish the difference between an actual thought and feeling. They will learn to be aware of how thoughts can influence their emotions and how it is sometimes unhelpful. They will also critically evaluate whether their automatic thoughts are accurate and have evidence, or if they are simply just biased. At the end of their therapy, they should have developed the skills to notice these negative thoughts, interrupt them, and correct the thoughts properly.

Now, let's talk about how other behavioral therapies are different. Most of them focus on how specific thoughts and behaviors are accidentally "rewarded" within an individual's environment. These rewards contribute to these thoughts and behaviors increasing. Behavior therapies assist with a wide selection of psychological symptoms in a wide range of ages. Here are a couple of examples to further explain it:

- Example #1:

Imagine a teenager who continually asks for permission to use the family car to hang out with friends. After the parents asking repeatedly and receiving numerous denials, the teenager becomes angry and disobedient towards the parents. Afterward, the parents conclude that they do not want to take the hassle from their teen anymore and allow their teen to borrow the car. By giving permission, the teenager has received a "reward" for throwing a tantrum. Behavior therapists say that by permitting the teenager, the teenager has learned that bad behavior is a strategy that works if they are going after permission. Moreover, behavior therapy aims to understand the relationships between behaviors, rewards, and learning and change negative patterns. In conclusion, the parents and children in this example can unlearn these unhealthy behaviors and reinforce good behavior instead.

- Example #2:

Imagine being afraid to ride in vehicles. To avoid being scared and anxious, you may eventually begin to avoid all vehicles and walk or ride a bicycle instead. The extra energy and time required for your transportation may cause you to be always late for events or work. Despite these consequences, however, your fear of riding in a car has been rewarded with an absence of fear and anxiety. Behavioral treatments would consist of riding in a car under a supervised environment and reward you when you are successful. These rewards come after each success, and it aims to help you unlearn these negative associations. Although behavioral therapies are different based on the disorder they are treating, a common thread is that behavioral therapists help their clients try new or feared behaviors and disallows them from letting negative rewards dictate their behavior.

A Blended Approach

We talked about the three main types of psychotherapy which is CBT, IPT, and psychodynamic therapy. There is another common approach- the blended approach. A blended approach could include either a blend of a few different psychotherapies or one kind of psychotherapy, including integrated talking therapies and digital content. For instance, while a person is going through CBT, they may be given homework through educational modules or apps to monitor their sleep or mood. This information usually helps the therapist have reflective conversations with the client.

Blended approaches of psychotherapy haven't fully developed or enmeshed into mental health services at the grand scale. Researchers are still studying the best methods to integrate digital content with the traditional face to face therapy, as well as how they can collect evidence on the effectiveness of it all. In a general sense, identifying barriers and facilitators for these digital methods has been a distinguishing line of work over recent years as this method is growing in popularity. For instance, some people may not have the means to pay for a therapist, so they can opt for CBT programs online or through a self-help book to self-direct their therapy and learning. This field is an excellent area of opportunity for researchers to study.

The Pros and Cons of CBT

In this section, we will look at CBT's pros and cons to give you an idea of the real-world benefits that it can provide you with and some of the challenges that come with it.

The Benefits of CBT

1. Studies have found research that shows that cognitive-behavioral therapy is as effective as medication in treating anxiety disorders and other mental health disorders.
2. CBT is time-sensitive - Completed in a short amount of time compared with other types of behavioral therapies.
3. CBT is highly structured, which means that therapists can conduct it in different formats. These formats include self-help books, groups, and computer programs.
4. During CBT, you learn valuable and practical skills that you can incorporate into your daily life. These skills can help you cope with current stresses and future difficulties as well.

The Drawbacks of CBT

1. To fully benefit from CBT, you need to commit to the process. A therapist can help and advise, but they cannot help solve your problems without your cooperation.
2. CBT's structured nature may not be suitable for people suffering from learning disabilities or more complex mental health problems.
3. Some people argue that CBT only helps with current problems and specific issues; it fails to address the possibility of underlying mental health issues. For example, an unhappy childhood.
4. CBT often focuses on the individual's ability to change their thoughts, feelings, and behaviors but does not address a more comprehensive set of problems regarding systems or families. These problems typically have a significant impact on somebody's health and wellbeing.

Overall, CBT is very useful in helping people manage their problems, such as depressive or anxious thoughts, to make it less likely to negatively impact a person's life. However, there is always a risk that the feelings you associate with your problems will return, but if you understand and know how to use your CBT skills, it should be easy for you to control them. If you practice CBT with a therapist or through a program, it is essential to practice your learned skills even when the sessions are over.

The Science Behind CBT

A constant theme in the later chapters of this book is that CBT is a complicated process, and it requires a lot of effort and commitment for the client to achieve the benefits. For those who are learning about cognitive behavioral therapy for the first time, homework and practice may be challenging and grueling at first. When people start CBT with their therapist, they will tell the client that they need to start very small with their initial changes. Like any habit that we develop, it takes a lot of time and self-discipline to get to the point where you don't have to think about it anymore.

In many cases, the first step and change you have to make using CBT is simply being aware of your thoughts. You don't necessarily have to try to change them yet, but you will begin to notice some unhealthy thinking styles you may have by starting to be aware of them.

The theory behind CBT is that an individual's thoughts, emotions, and behaviors are all connected. Creating small changes in your life will help you start to change your thoughts, which will influence a change in your emotions and behaviors. Here are a couple of tips on small changes you can make in your daily life:

- Balance your thoughts.

If you're suffering from a mental health disorder, you tend to have distressing and flawed thoughts, influencing your behavior. For example, if you get anxious in social situations, you tend to avoid them actively. Your mind automatically tells you that you would panic and do something embarrassing if you get yourself in a social situation. This belief would then reinforce your thoughts and avoidance of social situations. By balancing your thoughts, you begin to analyze your thought processes and see the error of your ways. By merely just paying attention to these automatic thoughts that lead to your beliefs, you may slowly be able to change your thought process, which would ultimately adjust your beliefs.

- Change your point of view.

Once you have established the ability to notice your thoughts simply, you can begin changing your perspective. By recognizing your cognitive distortions or unhelpful thinking styles, you can start to use a technique called cognitive restructuring to help transform your undesirable thoughts simply. In return, your behavior will change, as well. The next time you start to feel the emotions of anxiety, try asking yourself: "What thoughts am I having right now that are causing these emotions to arise?" By identifying the thoughts that are causing you distress, you can then restructure those thoughts to be helpful instead of problematic. As you notice the specific thoughts or memories causing you distress, you can write them down in a list. Writing them down will help you remember some recurring thoughts that then lead to negative emotions and behavior. Ultimately, this will help you understand how your thoughts are connected to your feelings and determine your trigger stimulus.

- Have patience with yourself.

As has been emphasized throughout this book, CBT takes time and hard work to pay off. Change can't happen overnight, so don't expect it to happen this way. Instead, your goal should be to develop the skills needed, so you feel ready to face any challenges your mental health throws at you! Be patient, and start small with your goals. Start by simply just paying attention to your thoughts when you feel a negative emotion. Set yourself up for small victories that will build you the confidence to start aiming for bigger goals. Be proud of any changes you begin to make even if they are small. Have patience with yourself, and try to recognize that progress isn't necessarily linear. You may have a more challenging time at a particular stage of CBT but an easier time during other stages.

- Be kind and gentle to yourself.

When suffering from mental health disorders, it is easy to get wrapped up in your negative self-talk without realizing it. However, continually feeling negative will not generate the confidence required to help yourself get better. Try to notice your negative thoughts like "Why do I never do anything right?" or "Other people don't struggle with this!" and replace these thoughts with something less harsh. Before you start judging yourself, ask yourself if your friend or family is in the same situation as you and having these thoughts, what would you say? Try to replace the ideas you have about yourself with the thoughts you would have towards other people. Doing this sounds easy to do, but the hard part is catching yourself when you fall into a negative spiral of self-judgment. Keep in mind that this doesn't mean you should be making excuses for yourself if you did make a mistake. However, this means that you should encourage yourself to stop the harsh self-judgment that you wouldn't use for other people.

- Do things that you love.

Mental disorders like anxiety and depression have a nasty way of stripping you away from things that you enjoy in life. Usually, it is because you have become scared of the possibility of failing at them or simply just lacking the motivation to pursue them. It could be as simple as having a love for reading, but you are too tired to do so. Make an active effort to schedule in time to do the things you love. While doing the things you love, try to make sure that you are being present and paying attention at the moment instead of letting your mind worry about the future or the past. Once you finish doing something that you love, ask yourself if it made you feel better. If so, this is a huge reason why you should be doing it regularly.

- Practice mindfulness.

In modern-day society, being mindful is a challenge due to the constant need to be doing something. You have probably experienced the feeling of laying in bed trying to go to sleep but find your mind thinking about a deadline at work or something that you said to your co-worker the other day. Regardless, these are all thoughts that are preventing you from being in the moment. Start small by trying to switch these thoughts away from events that aren't happening right now. Try asking yourself if your emotions are reflecting what is going on at that moment. If not, focus on your surroundings. Pay attention to how your body feels, the noises outside, the color of your walls. By being mindful, you are eliminating the possibility of negative automatic thoughts.

CHAPTER 3
What Can Cognitive Behavioral Therapy Treat?

Anxiety and depression are the most common disorders that people face in modern-day. The most common treatment for these disorders is Cognitive Behavioral Therapy (CBT). In addition to these two disorders, CBT can treat several other illnesses and conditions. In this chapter, we will look at the disorders that CBT can treat and how it can effectively treat them.

Psychologists originally developed CBT for the treatment of depression. Since then, CBT has been used to treat a variety of disorders in different settings. Over 250 analyses and research conducted over the last few decades, scientists found strong evidence in favor of using CBT for multiple types of mental disorders. While most of these studies focused on the adult population, some evidence supports CBT within children, adolescents, and the senior population.

What Is Depression?

You have likely heard of the term depression many times in your life. What exactly is depression? The dictionary definition of depression is *'feelings of severe despondency and dejection.'* Depression is a common buzzword and illness that people frequently talk about in the present-day. However, what does it mean? Somebody can feel 'depressed' as an emotion, but it does not necessarily mean that they have a mental disorder of depression. For starters, depression itself is also known as a major depressive disorder. It is a serious and common medical illness that affects the way people feel; it negatively affects them in most cases. Since depression heavily affects how a person feels, it also affects how they think and how they act. Luckily, depression is a treatable illness, and it is something that you can recover from using the right treatments.

Keep in mind that depression is not the same as feelings of sadness or grief. The death of a loved one or the ending of a relationship are both very difficult experiences for a person to experience and endure. It is entirely normal for feelings of sadness and grief to arise during these hard times in response to those situations. People who are experiencing an event of a loss might often describe themselves as being 'depressed.'

With that said, being sad is not the same as having the disorder of depression. A person's grieving process is unique to every individual, but it does share many of the same feelings that a depression disorder brings. Both depression and grief feelings involve feelings of sadness and withdrawal from a person's usual activities. Here are a few important ways that they are different:
- When a person is feeling emotions of grief, their painful feelings often come in waves. They usually mix with positive memories

about the person who's passed. When a person is feeling intense grief, their interest and mood decrease for around two weeks.
- When a person is in grief, their self-esteem usually does not change much. When a person has depression, they have constant feelings of self-loathing and worthlessness.
- For most people, the death of a loved one can cause major depression. For other people, it could be losing their job or being a victim of physical assault. When depression and grief are co-existing, the grief is usually the more painful feeling and lasts longer than grief without depression. There is some overlap between depression and despair, but despite this, they are still different. Helping a person distinguish between grief and depression is necessary to help them get help, support, or treatment.

Symptoms of Depression

One of the most essential parts of learning about how CBT can treat depression is first learning about the symptoms of depression. Understanding which symptoms depression causes can help people identify the difference between a period of grieving to an actual depression disorder. When a person feels sad, has negative thoughts, or has trouble sleeping, it does not necessarily mean that they have depression. For a person to be diagnosed with a depression disorder, they must be exhibiting these traits:
- The person's symptoms must be new to them or be noticeably worse compared to how they were before the depressive episode
- The person's symptoms must persist for most of the day and be as consistent as nearly every day for at least two consecutive weeks
- The episode that this person experiences also comes with impaired functioning or clinically significant distress

When you suspect that you may have a depression disorder, it is extremely important to discuss ALL of the symptoms you may be experiencing. The goal of depression treatments is to help people feel more like themselves again to enjoy the things they used to do. Professionals must find the right treatment to alleviate and address all their symptoms to achieve this peace of mind. Even if a person's doctor prescribes them medication suitable for their type of depression, this may take quite a bit of time. Some people must try different medicines until they find one that works best for their specific body. The goal of depression treatment is not only about getting better from it but also about staying better.

Throughout this book, we have to remember that depression is not a simple change of mood or a moment of 'weakness.' depression is a real medical condition that has many behavioral, physical, emotional, and cognitive symptoms. We will begin talking about all the different types of depression symptoms.

Emotional Symptoms

The most common symptoms of depression are emotional symptoms. These symptoms are the ones where you feel is affecting your state of mind. Here are examples of a few emotional symptoms that people with depression have to endure:

- **Constant sadness:** This symptom is the feeling of sorrow in a depressed person for no apparent reason. This feeling can feel very intense. It often feels like nothing can make it go away.
- **Feeling of worthlessness:** A person that is depressed often experiences unrealistic feelings of worthlessness or guilt. Usually, there isn't a specific event that provokes these feelings; they just happen at random.
- **Suicidal or dark thoughts:** These types of thoughts can occur very frequently during a person's depression. Therapists and professionals take these thoughts very seriously, and when a person is experiencing these emotions, they must ask for help right away.
- **Loss of interest or pleasure in activities that you previously enjoyed:** A depressed person may experience a loss of interest that affects all areas of their life. The loss of interest can range from not finding pleasure from their previous hobbies to everyday activities that the person used to enjoy.

Physical Symptoms

Physical symptoms play a considerable role in a person's depression. Usually, when people experience physical symptoms, they are close to discovering that they may have depression. Many people think that depression is limited to emotional symptoms, but this is untrue. Here are a few physical symptoms of depression:

- **Low energy:** People who have depression typically always feel low on energy even if they have not exerted themselves. This type of depressive fatigue is different because neither sleep nor rest can alleviate this tiredness.
- **Psychomotor impairment:** Depression can make a person feel as if everything slows down. This slowing includes slowed speech, body movement, thinking, speech in low volume, long pauses before answering, inflection, or muteness.
- **Aches and pains:** Depression can often cause physical pain. This pain includes joint pain, stomach pain, headaches, back pain, or other pains).
- **Insomnia or hypersomnia:** When a person is depressed, their sleep becomes broken and feels unrefreshing. When the person

wakes up, they are usually in a mental anguish that prevents them from falling back to sleep. Other cases can be the opposite where the person is excessively sleeping.
- **Change in weight:** A change in a person's weight is a significant sign for diagnosing depression.

Behavioral Symptoms

Besides emotional and physical symptoms, behavioral symptoms also play a considerable role in diagnosing depression. Some behavioral symptoms include:
- **Change in appetite:** The most common of all behavioral symptoms of depression is a decrease in appetite. People with depression report that food seems tasteless, and they think all servings are too large. Consequently, some people increase their food consumption instead, especially sweet foods, resulting in weight gain.
- **The impression of restlessness:** For some people, depression makes them very jumpy and agitated. They may struggle with sitting still, not pacing, fiddling with items, or hand-wringing.

Cognitive Symptoms

Cognitive symptoms are one of the least talked about symptoms when it comes to depression. This one is hard to diagnose, as many people don't know if they are experiencing it. The main cognitive symptom of depression is as follows:
- **Difficulty making decisions or focusing:** A depressed person may experience a lower ability to concentrate or think. This lowered concentration causes them to exhibit behaviors of indecisiveness.

Types of Depression

As we mentioned earlier, depression is different for everyone, and therefore, different people require different treatment methods. Depression isn't just one size fits all; it is a disorder that comes in many shapes and forms. When people get diagnosed with depression, doctors will define its severity by determining where its mild, moderate, or major. Determining this can be a complicated task, but knowing what type of depression you have can help you manage your symptoms and help you find the most effective depression to your specific type of depression. Let's learn about a few different types:

Mild and Moderate Depression

The most common types of depression are mild and moderate depression. This type of depression is more than just feeling 'sad' or 'blue' the symptoms of this type of depression often interferes with people's lives by robbing them of motivation and joy. These symptoms can feel amplified in moderate depression and often lower a person's self-esteem and self-confidence.

A type of 'low-grade' depression is called dysthymia. When a person has dysthymia, they feel mild to moderately depressed more often than not, but they do have brief periods of feeling a normal mood. Here are some defining traits of dysthymia:

- Symptoms of dysthymia are not as severe or strong as the symptoms of major depression, but they do tend to last for a long time (minimum of 2 years)
- Some people report that they experience intense depressive episodes on top of having dysthymia; this is a condition called 'double depression.'
- When a person is suffering from dysthymia, they may feel like they have always been depressed for their whole lives. They may think that their consistent low mood is 'just the way they are.'

Major Depression

Major depression is a less common form of mild or moderate depression; it involves severe and relentless symptoms. Here are two characteristics of major depression:

- If major depression is left untreated, it usually lasts for about six months
- Although some people only experience one depressive episode in their life, major depression can be a disorder that is recurring throughout their life

Atypical Depression

Atypical depression is a subtype of major depression that is very common that has specific symptom patterns. It has a better response with some medications and therapies than others, identifying this type of depression is very helpful when it comes to prescribing treatment. Here are a few traits to describe it further:

- Usually, atypical depression experiences a temporary increase in mood as a response to positive events. This increase in mood includes hanging out with friends or receiving some sort of good news.
- Atypical depression includes increased appetite, weight gain, sleeping excessively, sensitivity to rejection, and a 'heavy feeling' in their arms and legs.

Seasonal Affective Disorder (SAD)

Although many people think this type of depression is just a myth, it is a real condition. When they experience reduced daylight hours during winter, some people can cause them to form a type of depression called seasonal affective disorder (SAD). Although this is not a popular type of depression, SAD affects 1% - 2% of the general population, predominantly young people and women. SAD can make a person feel completely different from the person they are in the summer. People tend to feel stressed, sad, hopeless, tense, and have little interest in friends or activities they normally enjoy. SAD usually begins during Autumn or Winter, where the days are short and remains until Spring's brighter days come along.

The Science of Depression

One of the most important things for treating their depression is to get a very thorough understanding of it. Otherwise, they may blame their depression on other unhealthy factors, like their physical appearance, personality, social life, or lack of it. There are many theories behind what causes depression, but due to extensive research, this condition is mostly due to complex individual factors; the most widely accepted theory behind it is irregular brain chemistry.

Those who suffer from depression sometimes can relate their illness to a specific circumstance or event, for instance, something traumatic that has happened to them. However, it is also not unusual for people to wonder why they are depressed because they feel as if they don't have a reason to be. In both these cases, learning about the science and theories behind depression can help understand their version of depression.

Researchers in this field have theorized that for some people, depression can be caused by having not enough substances such as neurotransmitters in the human brain, and this can cause depression. Restoring some of these brain chemicals and finding a healthy balance can alleviate some people's depression symptoms. This balance is where medication such as antidepressants come in. We will discuss the different classes and types of antidepressants later on in this book.

This theory seems to be the simplest to tackle. I mean, it's just a matter of biology, math, and prescription that can get someone back on track, right? Wrong. Although it does seem simple, depression is an extremely complex condition to treat. Just because a person successfully treated their depression using medication, it doesn't mean that the next person can find success with the same method. Even a treatment method for someone who has worked successfully may slowly begin lower in effectiveness over time or even stop working completely. This lowered effectiveness happens for numerous reasons that scientists are still trying to comprehend. Researchers are still heavily invested in this area of science to continue to understand the mechanisms of depression more deeply, including chemicals in our brains, with the hope of finding more explanations and evidence for these complexities to continue developing more treatment methods for people.

Depression is still a multifaceted condition. However, simply having knowledge or awareness of the chemistry component in a person's brain proves to be very useful for mental health and medical professionals, and people suffering from depressive disorders. Below is a summary of the recognized science behind a depression disorder:

Neurotransmitters

For simplicity's sake, the chemical 'messengers' in our brain are called neurotransmitters. The nerve cells within our brain use these messengers, aka neurotransmitters, to communicate with one another. We believe that the messages that they send play a huge role in a person's mood regulation. The three neurotransmitters that are responsible for depression are:

- Dopamine
- Serotonin
- Norepinephrine

Besides these neurotransmitters, others also send messages in a person's brain. These include; GABA, acetylcholine, and glutamate. Scientists are still studying the specifics of what role these chemicals play in the brain when it comes to a person's depression or other mental conditions like fibromyalgia and Alzheimer's.

Let's learn a little about how our cells communicate with our neurotransmitters. A synapse is a space between two nerve cells. When two cells want to communicate with each other, our neurotransmitters can be packed up and then released from the cell for the destined cell to receive. As these packaged neurotransmitters travel across space, postsynaptic cells can take up those receptors to look for a specific chemical. For instance, serotonin receptors will aim to pick up serotonin molecules. If there are any excess lingering molecules in that space, the presynaptic cell will gather them and use them in another communication by reprocessing them. Different types of neurotransmitters carry different messages that play a specific role in creating a person's brain chemistry. Imbalanced in those chemicals are theorized to play a huge role in depression or other mental health conditions.

- Norepinephrine

Norepinephrine plays a dual purpose as a neurotransmitter and hormone. It is responsible for the 'fight or flight' response that humans feel, including adrenaline. It helps deliver messages between cells. In the 60s, scientists suggested that the chemical of interest was norepinephrine when it came to the human brain and depression. These scientists proposed "catecholamine" as the hypothesis of all mood disorders. They suggested that when there isn't enough norepinephrine in the human brain, that was when depression occurred. Otherwise, manic disorders occur when a person's brain has too much norepinephrine. Although there is plenty of evidence that supports this statement, many other researchers have challenged it. Firstly, they discovered that changes in norepinephrine levels do not affect every person's mood. Also, depression can be alleviated in some people by changing the levels of norepinephrine. Ultimately, researchers in the present-day now understand that low levels of norepinephrine are not the only chemical-cause of depression.

- Serotonin

Serotonin is one of the most well-known chemicals in the general population. Almost everybody knows that serotonin is the 'feel-good' chemical in a person's brain. Not only does serotonin help regulate a person's mood, but it also has a variety of different jobs in the human body ranging from blood clotting to sexual function. As it relates to depression, researchers have focused their time and efforts on serotonin over the past 20 years. This research has led to the invention of antidepressants like Prozac or other SSRIs, which is known as selective serotonin reuptake inhibitors. Just like the name SSRI states, these types of medication focus on acting upon serotonin molecules. A few famous doctors originally proposed that low levels of serotonin cause norepinephrine drop as well. Still, serotonin levels can be manipulated through the use of medication to raise norepinephrine. Another type of antidepressant, known as *Tricyclic antidepressants* (TCAs), can also affect serotonin and norepinephrine. However, they affect histamine and acetylcholine as well. TCAs' side effects include dry eyes, dry mouth, sensitivity to light, peculiar taste in the mouth, blurry vision, urinary hesitancy, and constipation. Consequently, SSRIs do not affect acetylcholine and histamine levels and don't offer TCAs' same side effects. Due to this, doctors and depressed people tend to opt for TCAs or different classes of antidepressants.

- Dopamine

The third chemical that has a huge role in a person's mood is dopamine. The chemical dopamine is also very well known, and people know that it is responsible for happiness and mood. Positive feelings related to reinforcement and reward are created by dopamine, helping people stay motivated to continue doing an activity or task. Scientists also believe that dopamine plays a big role in numerous conditions that involve the brain, including schizophrenia and Parkinson's. There is evidence that shows that lower dopamine levels contribute to depression in some people. When people go through many treatments that fail, doctors have prescribed medications that act like dopamine and found success. However, keep in mind that most medications used for depression usually take 6+ weeks to be effective. In our present-day, researchers are also focusing on finding out whether dopamine agents in medication can produce a faster result for treating depression. However, we must consider that there are a few severe disadvantages when using dopamine as medication. Dopamine is also encouraged to be produced by recreational drugs such as alcohol, opiates, and cocaine. It is not unheard of for people to self-medicate when they are depressed by using these substances. When someone activates their dopamine reward cycle through substance use, they can develop addictions as a result.

- Low Neurotransmitter Levels

Since we understand low levels of neurotransmitters cause depression, then our next question is, what exactly are the causes of low levels of norepinephrine, dopamine, or serotonin to begin with? Recent research has found a few potential causes of chemical imbalances in a person's brain. These causes could include:

- Not enough receptor sites available to receive neurotransmitters
- Not enough of a specific neurotransmitter is producing
- Not enough molecules that are responsible for building neurotransmitters
- Presynaptic cells are taking the neurotransmitters back up before it has the opportunity to be received by the destined cell
- The molecules that are responsible for making neurotransmitters are running out

An interruption anywhere in the total process can result in lower levels of neurotransmitters. Numerous new theories focus on the factors that cause low levels, for instance, mitochondrial stress. One of the main difficulties that doctors and researchers have in connecting low levels of brain chemicals to depression is that no method can consistently and accurately measure this. Other parts of the human body are also responsible for making neurotransmitters. These amounts need to be measured and considered when it comes to diagnosing depression and when looking for the most effective treatment method.

How Can CBT Be Used to Treat Depression

There is strong evidence that supports the use of CBT to treat depression at a moderate level. However, there isn't strong evidence that supports CBT as a treatment for more severe depression. The evidence for severe depression is mixed, but some studies suggest that CBT is as effective as medication.

That being said; however, CBT does still perform better for moderate depression compared to no treatment at all. Further, it performs better than other pharmaceutical or behavioral therapies. CBT is effective when it comes to preventing relapses as well.

As I mentioned, depression is a very complex disorder, and it reacts differently in each person that experiences it. There are also several different types of depression, as we saw above. For this reason, CBT is best used in combination with other treatment methods when it comes to treating depression. Each person should seek treatment and a therapist or doctor to find the treatment that works best for their case of depression.

What Is Anxiety?

The next disorder that CBT is effective in treating is anxiety. You have likely heard this work before, but what exactly is anxiety?
Often, when people use the term 'anxiety,' they are referring to generalized anxiety. Anxiety is a basic feeling and experience that every species of animal experiences. Although anxiety is not a pleasant feeling, it is not dangerous. Anxiety is helpful for us in certain situations. We all have to keep in mind that anxiety is a normal emotion and not dangerous. The symptoms of anxiety serve a function. Anxiety is a natural reaction to a perceived threat and helps us humans respond to it. However, if you have excessive anxiety, it can also be a problem.

The Most Common Causes of Anxiety

As you have just learned, a lot of the time, having one anxiety disorder can lead to a higher risk of developing others. Let's use OCD as an example. An individual suffering from OCD often feels a lot of shame and secrecy when it comes to their compulsive tendencies. A lot of the time, they don't want to showcase their tendencies around other people. This need to hide then creates a fear of being around other people. Having a fear of interacting and being around others is also a sign of a social disorder. If one anxiety disorder is left untreated for long periods, those symptoms will likely snowball into other ones.
All anxiety disorders have one thing in common; worry. Since worry is the largest component of anxiety and is responsible for generating anxiety, if someone is unable to manage their worry - they will likely become anxious and exhibit anxious behaviors. The worry that causes someone to develop GAD is the same worry that can cause someone to develop panic disorders. When someone is dealing with an overwhelming amount of worry, their environmental factors play a part in determining what type of disorder it manifests into. For instance, let's use two Bob and John as examples. Bob and John both experience the same amount of worry. Bob grew up in an environment where his parents exhibited excessive cleaning behaviors. John grew up in an environment where he was timid and never learned how to break out of his shyness. Assuming Bob and John are facing the same amount of worry is equal, Bob is likely to develop an obsessive-compulsive disorder because of his exposure to his parents' cleaning tendencies. However, John is likely to develop social anxiety disorder due to his childhood and the lack of help to work through his timid personality.
The common factor in anxiety disorders is the worry, which then manifests into anxiety. Environmental factors affect what these anxieties become, which affects what their behavior will be. As we discussed

earlier, those suffering from one anxiety disorder may develop another one if they don't treat the first within a reasonable time frame.

A common question that is asked often in modern-day society is, 'Is there an anxiety epidemic?" It seems like everywhere we go, and everyone we know is battling some sort of anxiety disorder. Media outlets are constantly talking about depression and anxiety, and chances are, a significant portion of people we know are using medication to battle their anxiety disorder(s). Are we being affected by the same forms of anxiety as our ancestors? The answer is that the way that anxiety manifests itself in people hasn't changed over time. We are still affected by the same forms of anxiety that affected our ancestors. However, the things that did change about anxiety are the triggers that we face. The traditional causes of anxieties that humans face are still prevalent today. For example, we still experience anxiety due to difficult relationships, bad health, poverty, disadvantage, and unemployment. Some of these traditional sources of anxiety are at an increase in the present day. These sources include; loneliness, undesirable relationship factors like divorce, or violence and abuse, childhood neglect, increased work stress and hours, and an overwhelming sense of lack of control over our lives. The lack of control is especially prevalent amongst the youth of our society who are being introduced to failure early on in their lives due to an increased systematic educational testing. Luckily, some of the most traditional anxiety sources, such as poverty and poor health, are on the decline. Still, it creates space for new anxieties, such as the stress of modern-day jobs and income inequality.

Moreover, modern technology and media have created an entirely new set of anxiety sources for the present generations. Yes, we are talking about social media. The need to have 24/7 connectivity, the need to multitask various activities at all times, and the need to keep up with news alerts and doomsday scenarios. Soon, almost every single appliance in our homes will have internet connectivity to grant you access to social media to keep you online. This increase in connectivity will increase the fears of data hacking, identity theft, trolling, phishing, and even grooming. Even our simple computers bring in daily anxieties that include; forgotten passwords, hard drive crashes, and daily digital transactions. All transactions start to feel very distant when they are all done through technology. A lot of the time, all you want is to just speak to a real person. Did you know that most children under the age of 20 have never lived without social media to build off of social media anxiety? The present research has associated social media use with social anxiety. The research proposes that social anxiety and loneliness can generate feelings of disconnectedness when we are constantly viewing the rich and successful lives of others. Another consequence of social media use is that the youth track their social success and status using metrics like the number of followers or friends they have on their social media. The metrics are different from the traditional way people counted how many real genuine friends they had.

On top of the numerous new and modern anxieties, there is an increasing social culture shift regarding anxiety. This change has been very contradictory in terms of the messages it sends to society. We constantly hear that anxiety is an appropriate feeling in response to the modern-day stresses. Anxiety is almost a sort of status symbol that showcases how successful and busy you are. However, we also hear that having too much anxiety requires treatment. The diagnosis of different categories of anxiety has exploded over the past thirty years. The pharmaceutical industry has never been keener to medicalize anxiety so they can sell us a pharmaceutical fix for it. This fix led to numerous social campaigns over the years to bring awareness to mental health disorders (e.g., depression and anxiety) to destigmatize it, diagnose it, and seek medical treatment for it.

Although our anxiety epidemic sounds dooming, it is not entirely the case. According to research, 20% of people suffer from extremely high anxiety levels, but no evidence supports the growth of this ratio. If the ratio remains at 20%, due to our population's growth, the number of people suffering from anxiety will grow too. As more people face anxiety disorders, more people will be seeking treatment for it as we continue to bring awareness to mental health. On the other hand, 40% of people experience low anxiety levels and will not be motivated to seek treatment unless they go through a very distressing event or period of their life.

The Science of Anxiety

Since anxiety is a normal response to a threat, when a person perceives that they are threatening, this triggers their fight or flight instinct. Its sole purpose is to protect itself by fighting or fleeing from danger. When somebody feels threatened, their brain sends messages to your autonomic nervous system (this is a section of your nerves). When this nervous system reacts, it releases adrenalin and noradrenalin from the brain, which then triggers the anxiety response and automatically prepares us for danger. This nervous system eventually stops when our bodies destroy these chemicals to calm the body down.

This fact is extremely important to remember because those who suffer from anxiety disorders believe that their anxiety will go on forever. However, biologically this cannot happen since the body limits anxiety over time. Although it may feel that the anxiety is going on forever, it has a limited lifespan. After some time, your body will determine that it has had enough with the fight or flight instinct and restore the body to its neutral feeling. Anxiety cannot continue endlessly or damage your body. Although highly uncomfortable, this whole cycle is perfectly harmless and natural. This behavior is instinct to us because, in the wild, it is necessary for our bodies to reactivate this response. After all, we know that danger can return.

Overall, the "fight or flight" response activates the entire body's metabolism. This response makes someone feel hot, flushed, and tired afterward because the entire process uses up a lot of energy. After a strong anxiety experience, most people feel drained, tired, and completely worn out.

Anxiety Disorders

Now that you know what anxiety is and how it is a natural emotion that we feel for protection - what is an anxiety disorder? An anxiety disorder is a medical condition where the individual feels symptoms of extreme anxiety or panic. In other words, an anxiety disorder is when the individual is feeling severe anxiety or panic and is unable to manage their symptoms.

We will be going through all the different types of anxiety disorders in another subchapter, but in this one, we will be talking about the most common ones that people face nowadays. The most common anxiety disorder that people face in the present-day is Generalized Anxiety disorder.

Symptoms of Anxiety Disorders

Diagnosing anxiety is far from simple. Unlike physical illnesses, it is not caused by a germ or bacteria that we can detect in a blood test. Anxiety manifests in numerous forms and can also be a symptom of other existing medical conditions. To properly diagnose anxiety, you need to complete a physical examination. This examination will allow your doctor to determine if other health issues cause your anxiety symptoms or if your anxiety is masking other symptoms. Usually, a complete personal health history is needed to make a complete diagnosis.

A rule of thumb is that you need to be 100% honest with the doctor making your diagnosis. Multiple things contribute to or can be affected by anxiety. These factors include:
- Hormones
- Specific Illnesses
- Coffee and/or alcohol consumption
- Medications

Certain medical conditions can also cause symptoms that appear like anxiety. Physical anxiety symptoms include:
- Shortness of breath
- Racing heart
- Sweating
- Shaking
- Chills or hot flashes
- Nausea

- Chest pain
- Vomiting
- Diarrhea
- Frequent urination
- Dry mouth

Your doctor will likely perform a variety of physical exams on you to help rule out possible medical conditions that mimic anxiety symptoms. Medical conditions that share similar symptoms with anxiety are:
- Asthma
- Heart attack
- Withdrawal related to substance abuse
- Side effects of diabetes or high blood pressure drugs
- Withdrawals from drugs used to treat sleep disorders or anxiety
- Hyperthyroidism
- Menopause
- Angina

Your doctor may suggest that you complete self-assessment questionnaires before you complete another testing after ruling out medical conditions. This assessment can help you recognize whether you have an anxiety disorder or react to a distressing event or situation. If the self-assessments result in the possibility of an anxiety disorder, your doctor may recommend you take a clinical assessment or have a structured interview with you.

Generalized Anxiety Disorder (GAD)

Generalized anxiety is the susceptibility to excessive panic, worry, or anxiety regarding numerous events or situations. Usually, the person has major difficulty controlling their feelings of worry and is associated with other symptoms such as fatigue, restlessness, concentration difficulties, sleep disturbance, irritability, and muscle tension. We define the feeling of worry as a process focused on the uncertainty of the outcome regarding future events. It is not an emotion itself, but it leads to feeling the emotion of anxiety. The main and most obvious symptom of generalized anxiety disorder is the "what if" thoughts that begin to occur. These "what if" thoughts work hand in hand with worrying, and it often feels like it is uncontrollable. Also, the process of worry is often associated with physical symptoms that are related to the flight or fight response. It often happens that the individual will think of the future negatively and have thoughts that are followed by feelings of anxiety.

People with GAD often feel worried and anxious most of the time and not just in specific stressful situations. The worries that they have been constant, intense, and interferes with their daily routine. Their worries are typically multiple aspects and not only one. It may include work, health, finance, family, or just everyday life things. Trivial tasks such as household chores or being late for a meeting can lead to extreme anxiety, leading to doom.

Most people are diagnosed with GAD if they showcase some of the symptoms for six months or more:
- You feel extremely worried about numerous activities or events.
- You struggle to stop worrying.
- You are finding that your anxiety has made it very hard for you to do your daily routine (e.g., studying, working, hanging out with friends)
- You constantly feel restless or on edge.
- You are always/easily tired.
- You struggle with concentration.
- You are easily irritable.
- You have tension in your muscles (e.g., neck or sore jaw)
- You struggle with sleeping (e.g., difficulty staying asleep or falling asleep)

About 14% of the population suffers from GAD in the present day. This condition tends to appear in more women than men and can occur at any time in an individual's life. It is common in all age groups, even including young children and seniors. However, the most common time for diagnosis is when an individual is around 30 years of age. Children who suffer from GAD will usually have exhibit behaviors like:
- Being un-confident of themselves
- Being over-conforming
- They are seeking constant approval and assurance from others.
- Being a perfectionist
- Needing to re-do tasks to perfection
- Using the phrase "Yes, but what if?"

So what exactly causes GAD? This one is tricky; there is a combination of different factors that take place. First, we consider biological factors. GAD is associated with certain changes in brain functions. Next, we also consider family history. Often, people who have GAD have a history of mental health issues in their family. Stressful life events also increase the risk of someone developing GAD. For example, loss of a relationship, moving, or physical or emotional abuse are all examples of events that can play a role in causing GAD. Lastly, psychological factors may also put a person at higher risk. Those who have personality traits of being sensitive, nervous, or inability to tolerate frustration are at higher risk of GAD.

The most common treatment for GAD is Cognitive Behavioral Therapy. You can turn to medication if psychological treatments are ineffective. We will be diving into the later chapters on why and how CBT is an extremely effective treatment for those who have GAD.

Other Types of Anxiety Disorders

Now that we have learned about the most common anxiety disorder, generalized anxiety disorder (GAD), and the largest component that leads to it (worry), we will learn about other types of anxiety disorders that people suffer from. The other types of anxiety disorders that we will learn about are:
- Social Anxiety
- Specific Phobias
- Panic Disorder
- Obsessive-Compulsive Disorder (OCD)
- Post-traumatic Stress Disorder (PTSD)

People who experience anxiety often showcase symptoms of more than one type of anxiety disorder. It's important to learn about these early on to help identify the symptoms to get treatment early on. Usually, the symptoms that you may experience do not go away on their own, and if they are left untreated, they can begin to take over your daily life.

- Social Anxiety

Although it is very normal to feel a certain level of nervousness in social situations, it is not normal to feel overwhelming anxiety. Situations such as attending formal events, public speaking, and doing presentations are likely events in which you feel nervous and anxious. However, for those who suffer from social anxiety (or otherwise known as social phobia), speaking or performing in front of other people and general social situations can lead to extreme anxiety. This anxiety usually stems from the fear of being criticized, judged, humiliated, or laughed at in front of other people. A lot of the time, they are afraid of trivial and ordinary matters. For example, those who suffer from social anxiety may feel that eating at a restaurant around other people can be extremely daunting.

Social anxiety usually occurs during the lead up to performance events (e.g., having to give a speech or working while people are watching them) and situations where social interaction is involved (e.g., having lunch with coworkers or normal small talk). Social anxiety also occurs during the actual event and the lead-up. Moreover, this type of phobia can also be very specific where the individual fears a specific situation. For example, they can be fearful of having to be assertive during work meetings.

The symptoms of social anxiety include psychological and physical symptoms. People with social phobia find it very distressing when they experience physical symptoms. These physical symptoms include:
- Excessive perspiration
- Nausea/Diarrhea
- Trembling
- Stammering, stuttering, or blushing when speaking

When these physical symptoms occur, it normally causes the anxiety to increase as the person begins to fear that other people will notice these signs. However, these signs are usually not noticeable to other people.

Those who suffer from this condition say that they also excessively worry that they will say or do something wrong, which will lead to a terrible result. Often, people with social anxiety will attempt to avoid situations where they feel like they can act in an embarrassing or humiliating way. If they can't avoid certain situations, they will choose to endure it but will become very distressed and anxious and try to exit that situation as fast as possible. This enduring can begin to harm their relationships. Moreover, it may begin to affect their professional lives and their ability to maintain their daily routine.

We base a typical social anxiety diagnosis on having the symptoms mentioned above and how much distress and impairment it causes on the individual's day-to-day routine. Usually, if symptoms continue for six months or more, then the doctor will make a diagnosis.

Some social phobia symptoms that are psychological include:
- They are feeling extreme nervousness before performing in front of other people.
- They are feeling extreme nervousness before meeting unfamiliar people.
- They are feeling extreme nervousness or embarrassment when being observed (e.g., eating or drinking in front of others, talking on the phone in front of others)
- They are not going to certain events or interactions due to the fear of social nervousness.
- They are having difficulty going about daily life (e.g., studying, seeing friends, and working)

Research suggests that 11% of the population has experienced social anxiety in their lifetime. It showed that women experience this disorder more than men. A lot of the time, this phobia starts during childhood or adolescence.

So, what exactly causes social anxiety? There are numerous causes, but the most common ones are temperament, family history, and learned behavior. When it comes to temperament, children or adolescents who are shy are at more risk than others. Specifically, for children, those who exhibit shyness and timidity puts them at risk of developing social anxiety in their adulthood. Family history is also a possibility when it comes to cause due to genetic predisposition. The leading cause, however, is usually learned behavior. Often, those who suffer from social anxiety develop this condition due to being treated poorly, embarrassed in public, or humiliated.

When it comes to treating social phobia, psychological treatments will be the first line of treatment, and in more severe cases, medication can be effective. Since social phobia is a type of anxiety disorder, many professionals choose to use Cognitive Behavioral Therapy as a treatment

method. Later on in this book, we will be talking about how CBT helps treat anxiety disorders.
- Phobias

Phobias are probably one of the most well-known disorders that we hear about in present-day society. You probably see people on TV and movies that have phobias of clowns, spiders, or heights. Fear or concern regarding certain situations is common, but that does not mean you have a phobia. Feeling anxious when you come across a spider or being in a high place is relatively normal. Fear is a rational and natural response when we are in situations where we feel threatened.

However, some people have a huge reaction to certain activities, situations, or objects due to them imagining and exaggerating the danger. The feelings of terror, panic, or fear that someone may feel due to a threat are entirely out of proportion. In many cases, even a thought of the phobic stimulus or seeing it on TV is enough to cause a reaction in these individuals. These types of extreme reactions could indicate a specific phobia disorder.

Although people are not self-aware of where their anxiety is coming from, people who suffer from phobias are usually aware that their fears are irrational and extreme. However, they do feel that their reactions are automatic and that they cannot control them. Sometimes, specific phobias lead to panic attacks. During these panic attacks, the individual finds themselves overwhelmed with undesirable physical sensations. These sensations include nausea, heart racing, choking, chest pain, dizziness, faintness, and hot/cold flashes.

The symptoms of specific phobia are as follows:
- You have a constant, extreme, and irrational fear of a situation, activity, or object. For example, you have a fear of heights, clowns, or spiders.
- You are constantly avoiding situations where there is a possibility that you have to face your phobia—for example, not going outside because you may encounter a spider. If the situation is difficult to avoid, you may start to feel high levels of distress.
- You find that your avoidance and anxiety of certain situations where your phobia might exist makes it hard for you to go about your daily routine. For example, it begins to interfere with your work, school, or social life.
- You find that your avoidance and anxiety are constant, and you have been struggling with it for over six months.

We can split specific phobias into the following categories:
- Animals: Your fear is related to animals or insects (e.g., fear of cats or spiders)
- Natural environment: Your fear is related to the natural environment (e.g., fear of heights or lightning)
- Injury/injection: Your fear is related to invasive medical procedures (e.g., fear of needles or seeing blood)

- Situations: Your fear is related to very specific situations (e.g., riding an escalator or driving in heavy traffic)
- Other: Your fear is to over miscellaneous phobias (e.g., fear of throwing up or fear of choking)

The first sign of specific phobia symptoms usually come up during childhood or early adolescence. Fear is quite normal amongst children, and they experience a lot of common fears during their childhood. Common fears are; being afraid of strangers, imaginary monsters, the dark, and animals. However, learning to manage these fears properly is part of the process of growing up. Some children can still develop specific phobias to the severity of panic attacks. These children have a higher risk to develop specific phobias compared to the other types of anxiety disorders. In most cases, children are not aware of the fact that their fears are extreme and irrational.

So, what exactly causes specific phobias besides anxiety? Like social anxiety, a person's temperament and history of mental health conditions play a huge role in the causation of specific phobias. Phobias are very treatable, and we use psychological treatments like CBT first to tackle the disorder. In cases where specific phobia is more severe, medication will be involved to help with the disorder.

- Panic Disorder

Panic disorder, or more commonly known as 'panic attacks,' is the term used to describe when these attacks are recurring and disabling. Usually, panic disorders are defined by:

- Unexpected and recurring panic attacks.
- You worry for a long duration (1 month+) after having a panic attack that you will have another one.
- You are worried about the effects or consequences after that panic attack. A lot of people will think that a panic attack is a symptom of an undiagnosed medical issue. For instance, individuals may do repeated medical tests due to these worries, and although nothing shows up, they still are afraid of being in poor health.
- You have significant behavior changes linked to the panic attacks—for example, avoiding exercise because your heart rate will increase.

Usually, during a panic attack, you become overwhelmed with the physical feelings described above. The panic attack peak is usually 10 minutes in and will last up to 30 minutes and leave you exhausted afterward. They can occur up to numerous times a day or a few times per year. They can happen when someone is sleeping, which will wake them up during the attack. Many people have experienced a panic attack at least one time in their lives. Up to 40% of the human population has experienced a panic attack at some point in their lives. This statistic does not mean you have a panic disorder. Here are the common symptoms and signs of a panic attack:

- A feeling of overwhelming fear or panic

- You have the thought that you are choking, dying, or 'going crazy.'
- Heart rate increases
- Having difficulty breathing (e.g., hyperventilating)
- Feeling like you are choking, or your lungs aren't working.
- Perspiring excessively
- Light-headedness, dizziness, or faintness

In some cases, a person going through a panic attack can also experience 'dissociation' or 'derealisation.' This is the sensation where you feel like the world and the environment around you is not real. This symptom is associated with the intense physiological changes in the body during this anxiety attack.

Panic disorders are not as common as other disorders such as GAD or social anxiety. Shockingly, 5% of the population have experienced panic disorder within their lifetime. According to statistics, women are more prone to a panic disorder than men. Panic disorders typically occur when people are in their early to mid-20s or in their mid-life. Panic disorders can occur at any age, but they are extremely rare in children or older people.

So what exactly causes a panic disorder? Although there isn't a specific cause, multiple factors are usually involved. Included could be people with a family history of anxiety disorders or depression. Some studies even suggest that genetics plays a big role. Biological factors are also associated with panic disorders such as; asthma, irritable bowel syndrome (IBS), and hyperthyroidism. Negative experiences in life also play a huge role in panic disorders. Severely stressful life experiences like sexual abuse or bereavement sometimes lead to panic disorders. Moreover, individuals going through extreme ongoing stress are at a high risk of developing panic disorders.

When it comes to treatments for panic disorders, the treatments reduce panic attacks from those who suffer from it. We give those suffering from severe panic disorder medication to help calm them, but psychological treatments like CBT will be the first method used.

- Obsessive-Compulsive Disorder (OCD)

As we discussed in our subchapter about worry, worrying thoughts can lead to anxiety, influencing our behavior. This influence can be helpful at times. For example, thinking that you may have left your stove on will lead you to check on it to ensure you are keeping things safe. However, if that thought becomes recurring and obsessive, it begins to influence unhealthy behavior patterns that cause the daily routine to be difficult. An example of OCD is repeatedly checking the stove to make sure they turned it off, even though you have already confirmed it the first time.

Often, people who suffer from OCD feel extreme shame about their need to carry out their compulsive actions. These feelings of shame cause secrecy, which then leads to delayed diagnosis and treatment. It can often result in a social disability where children fail to go to school or adults failing to leave their homes.

So, what are the signs and symptoms of Obsessive-Compulsive Disorder? OCD usually occurs in different types:

- Cleanliness and Order: Examples include obsessive household cleaning or hand-washing to mitigate the fear of contamination or germs, obsession with symmetry or order, and an excessive need to place objects or perform tasks in a specific pattern or place.
- Counting and Hoarding: Examples include repeatedly counting objects such as bricks on the wall, counting their clothes, or hoarding useless items like old newspapers or garbage.
- Safety: This is an obsessive fear about harm occurring to loved ones or themselves and can lead to impulsively checking on things to make sure they have turned everything off, and entrances are locked.
- Sexual Issues: Having an irrational fear or disgust regarding any sexual activity.
- Religious and Moral Issues: Feeling the need or compulsion to pray numerous times a day to the point where it affects their relationships and work.

When it comes to symptoms of OCD, beware of looking out for:

- Having repetitive concerns or thoughts that are about more than just regular life problems (e.g., having thoughts that something will harm your loved ones or that something will harm you)
- Doing the same activity in a very ordered and repeated manner each time. Examples include:
    - You constantly shower, brush your teeth, wash your clothes, or your hands.
    - You constantly rearrange tidy or clean things in a particular way at home or at work.
    - You constantly check that you locked all entrances and that you turned off all electronics.
- You feel relieved after doing those tasks but soon after feeling the need to repeat them.
- Being aware that these feelings, behaviors, and tendencies are unreasonable cannot help it.
- You are finding that these behaviors and thoughts interfered with your daily routine and took up more than one hour a day.

OCD is not as common as the other disorders we have discussed. Only around 3% of the population has experienced OCD in their lifetime. OCD can occur at any stage in your lifetime, and even children as young as six years old may showcase symptoms. However, symptoms only develop fully when the individual reaches their adolescence.

Based on research, we theorize OCD to have developed from a mix of environmental factors and genetics. Multiple other factors can increase the risk of developing OCD, including social factors, psychological factors, and family history. We link biological factors such as neurological issues and irregular levels of serotonin to OCD. There is active research right now regarding how structural, chemical, and functional changes in the brain may lead to OCD. Also, learned behaviors and environmental factors can cause OCD to develop. It can happen through direct conditioning or watching the behaviors of others. Since children are very impressionable, they will have a higher risk of developing OCD in their adolescence by watching their parents' compulsive behaviors.

OCD is usually treated by psychological treatments like CBT first, but we also use medication because many cases are more severe. In certain cases, a combination of medication and psychological treatments like therapy will be used at the same time to increase effectiveness.

- Post-Traumatic Stress Disorder (PTSD)

People who have been through a traumatic situation or event that has threatened their safety, life, or the life of others can develop a set of undesirable reactions called PTSD. These traumatic situations could be anything from a car accident to war to natural disasters like an earthquake. As a result of these traumatic events, the person will have intense horror, fear, or helplessness.

Individuals who have PTSD will often have feelings of intense fear or panic, very similar to those they felt during that traumatic situation. There are four main types of difficulties within PTSD:

- Re-living the traumatic situation/event: The individual constantly re-lives the traumatic situation or event through memories; often, this takes place in the form of imagery and nightmares. This re-living can also lead to extreme physical and emotional reactions like panic, heart palpitations, or sweating.
- Being extremely alert: The individual experiences concentration issues, irritability, and insomnia. They are easily scared and startled and are always looking out for signs of danger.
- Avoiding reminders of the situation/event: The individual purposely avoids places, activities, people, emotions, or thoughts related to the traumatic event because they bring back distressing memories.
- Feeling emotionally numb: This individual has lost interest in daily activities, feels isolated from family and friends, or feeling emotionally numb.

It is quite common for people who have PTSD also to experience other types of anxiety disorder. These other disorders could have been developed as a response to the traumatic event or developed after PTSD itself. The common additional disorders that this individual may face include depression, GAD, and drug or alcohol abuse.

If someone has gone through a traumatic event that involved injury, abuse, torture, or death, then they may experience the following symptoms of PTSD:
- Flashbacks of memories or dreams of the event
- If reminded of the event, you become physically and psychologically distressed.
- You have trouble remembering significant parts of that event.
- You have a negative perspective on yourself or other people.
- You constantly blame yourself or other people for that event.
- You constantly feel the emotions of anger, guilt, or shame.
- You no longer have an interest in the things you used to enjoy
- You feel like you are cutting yourself off from other people.
- You struggle with feeling positive emotions, such as excitement or love.
- You struggle with sleeping (e.g., insomnia or nightmares)
- You are easily angered or irritated.
- You find yourself engaging in recklessness and self-destructive behavior.
- You struggle with concentrating.
- You are always alert or vigilant.
- You get startled easily.

If someone feels more than four symptoms above for a month or more, they likely have PTSD. PTSD is something that anyone can develop following a traumatic event. However, those at greater risk are normally involved in deliberate harm like physical or sexual assault. Besides the event itself, other factors of developing PTSD include having a history of mental health problems, an ongoing stressful life, or lack of social support.

Around 12% of the population has experienced PTSD in their lifetime. In the western world, serious accidents are the leading causes of PTSD. If you are someone who has just gone through a traumatic event and is feeling very distressed, start by talking to your family doctor to get diagnosed. The earlier that you implement treatment, the more effective it is in helping you.

When it comes to PTSD treatment, many people recover on their own or through friends and family support. Due to this statistic, medical treatment doesn't usually begin until at least two weeks after the traumatic event. Although formal treatment is usually not offered right away, it is important that the first few days following the event that you go to and seek help and support. The support from family and friends is crucial for most people going through trauma. Minimizing other stressful life events helps the individual focus more of their time and effort on their recovery. Treatments for PTSD usually start with psychological treatment, such as talking therapies like CBT. In some severe cases, medication will be prescribed but are usually not recommended with PTSD.

How Can CBT Treat Anxiety Disorders?

Most of the research and practices to date support the use of CBT for the treatment of anxiety. CBT is very effective in treating anxiety disorders such as; social anxiety, generalized anxiety, and PTSD. It is also proven to be effective for less common disorders such as phobias and OCD. The National Institute for Health and Care Excellence (NICE) recommends Cognitive Behavioral Therapy to be the first approach to treating anxiety disorders.

CBT has been introduced to numerous countries and has established successful programs. However, even with the newest treatments, we are still a long way from helping 100% of people recover from mental disorders. Disorders such as GAD and OCD can be lifelong debilitating conditions. GAD and OCD are very resistant in some cases, even when exposed to medications and multiple psychotherapies. The only way to help more people who are suffering from anxiety disorders is to keep funding research to refining and developing therapies.

Some people wish to get rid of anxiety completely, but that goal isn't possible or realistic! When it comes to Cognitive Behavioral Therapy, the approach is to help you build the skills required to help you manage and understand your anxiety instead of getting rid of it altogether (again, not possible).

- Stress-Related Disorders

The most harmful type of stress is chronic stress. When it is left untreated for an extended amount of time, chronic stress can cause damage that can damage your physical and mental health irreversibly. For instance, poor work environments, long-term poverty, unemployment, repeated abuse in any form, dysfunctional family, or an unhappy marriage can cause a person significant chronic stress. When a person feels hopeless and does not see any way out of it and gives up entirely on finding solutions, chronic stress can set in and begin affecting their physical and mental health. When a person continuously lives with chronic stress, their emotional and behavioral actions can become ingrained. The wiring of their brains and bodies begins to change and makes them more prone to the negative effects that stress has on a person's body regardless of what's happening to them.

Types of Stress

Chronic stress is a grinding type of stress because it wears people down day after day. It negatively impacts the body and mind significantly and has the power to change a person forever. Chronic stress can be so dangerous that it can kill people due to suicide, heart attacks, strokes, and even cancer. There are treatment practices that can help people manage their chronic stress, but it requires them to be actively practicing those techniques throughout their lives. Later in this book, we will be exploring numerous treatment methods for stress disorders and related disorders caused by stress. If you think you are someone that is suffering from chronic stress, get help right away. Seek professional opinion and get it diagnosed; that will be the first step in discovering what methods are most suitable for your type of stress.

In some cases, you may not even have chronic stress and just another type of stress. In that case, you can use different methods and techniques to manage them properly. Next up in this chapter, we will be looking at the general symptoms of stress. This section will help you identify whether or not you feel like you have a stress disorder.

Symptoms of Stress

- Acne
- Headaches
- Chronic Pain
- Frequent Sickness
- Insomnia
- Decreased Energy
- Decreased Libido
- Digestive Issues
- Appetite Changes
- Depression
- Rapid Heartbeat
- Sweating

How CBT Can Help With Stress-Related Disorders

When a person is under a lot of stress for an extended amount of time, it increases their risk of developing other mental disorders. Common disorders that can be caused by high stress include; anxiety, depression, anger disorders, and panic disorders. We have already discussed several of these disorders in this chapter, and how CBT can treat them. It is important to note that if you are under high stress, learning what disorders chronic stress can lead to may help you identify it or learn to cope with your struggles related to stress.

How CBT Can Help With Other Disorders

As you know, CBT teaches a person to look within themselves and understand themselves better.
Several types of emotional deficiencies or causes can lead a person to develop disordered mental processes, resulting in various mental health disorders. We will explore some of these factors in hopes that you will recognize some of the reasons why you may experience struggles with your mental health.

Childhood Causes

The first example of an emotional deficiency that we will examine is more of an umbrella term for various emotional deficits. This umbrella term is Childhood Causes.

If you think back on your childhood, think about how your relationships began in your early life. Maybe you were taught that when you behaved, you received food as a reward. Perhaps when you were feeling down, you were given food to cheer you up. Maybe you turned to food when you were experiencing adverse events that happened during your childhood. Another cause could be the relationship you had with your parents in your formative years. Maybe you grew up in an emotionally abusive home, and food was the only comfort you had. These reasons are entirely valid, and this was the only way you knew how to deal with problems when you were a child. The positive thing is that now that you are an adult, you can take control of your life and make lasting changes for the better.

This example illustrates how mental struggles can lead to disordered eating, and they can also lead to more serious struggles such as depression or anxiety.

These experiences could cause someone to suffer from emotional disorders in adulthood, as it becomes something learned from an early age. This type of emotional deficiency is quite challenging to break as it has likely been a habit for many, many years, but it is possible.

When we are children, we learn habits and make associations without knowing it that we often carry into our later lives. While this is no fault of yours, recognizing it as a potential issue is important to make changes.

Covering Up Emotions

Another emotional deficiency that can manifest itself in adulthood is the effort to cover up our emotions.

Sometimes we would rather distract ourselves and cover up our feelings than to feel them or to face them head-on. In this case, our brain may try to distract us from feeling our true feelings.

When we have a quiet minute where these feelings or thoughts pop into our minds, we can cover them up by deciding to prepare food and eat and convince ourselves that we are "too busy" to acknowledge our feelings because we have to deal with our hunger. Further, we may distract ourselves by playing video games or surrounding ourselves with people. The fact that hunger often arises in this scenario makes it very difficult to ignore and very easy to deem as a necessary distraction. After all, we do need to eat to survive.

This distraction can be a problem, though if we do not need nourishment we are telling ourselves that this is why we cannot deal with our demons or our emotions. If you think you may be avoiding dealing with or thinking about or thinking about or thinking about or if you tend to be very uncomfortable with feelings of unrest, you may be experiencing this type of emotional eating.

CHAPTER 4
Cbt And Unhelpful Thinking Styles

To understand CBT effectively, we must understand the different types of unhelpful thinking styles that exist in people with the disorders that it treats to understand how it can treat them.

What Are Unhelpful Thinking Styles?

Below are the twelve types of cognitive distortions that you need to learn:
1. All or nothing thinking
This kind of thinking is otherwise known as 'black and white thinking.' You tend to see things in either black or white or success or failure. If your performance is not perfect, you will see it as a failure.
2. Overgeneralization
You see one single negative situation as a pattern that never ends. You draw conclusions of future situations based on one single event.
3. Mental filter
You choose one single undesirable detail, and you exclusively dwell on it. Your perception of reality becomes negative based on it. You only notice your failures, but you don't look at your successes.
4. Disqualifying the positive
You discount your positive experiences or success by saying, "that doesn't count." By discounting all your positive experiences, you can maintain a negative perspective even if you find it contradictory to your daily life.
5. Jumping to conclusions
You make a negative assumption even when you don't have supporting evidence. There are two types of jumping to conclusions:
(1) Mind reading: You imagine that you already know what other people are thinking negatively of you, and therefore you don't bother to ask.
(2) Fortune-telling: You predict that things will end up badly, and you convince yourself that your prediction is a fact.
6. Magnification/Minimization
You blow things out of proportion or inappropriately shrink something to make it seem unimportant. For example, you beef up somebody else's achievement (magnification) and shrug off your own (minimization).
7. Catastrophizing
You associate terrible and extreme consequences to the outcome of situations and events. For example, if someone rejects you for a date, it means that you are alone forever, and making an error at work means your boss will fire you.
8. Emotional reasoning
You assume that your negative emotions reflect the reality. For example, "I feel it so, therefore, it is true."
9. "Should" statements

You motivate yourself using terms like "should" and "shouldn't" as if you associate a reward or punishment before you do anything. Since you associate a reward or a punishment with "I should" or "I shouldn't," when other people don't follow it, you feel anger or frustration.

10. Labeling and mislabeling

This kind of thought is an example of overgeneralization to the extreme. Instead of describing your mistake, you automatically associate a negative label to yourself, "I'm a loser." You also do this to others; if someone else's behavior is undesirable, you attach "they are a loser" to them as well.

11. Personalization

You take responsibility for something that wasn't your fault. You see yourself as the cause of an external situation.

12. All at once, bias

This type of thinking is when you think risks and threats are right at your front door, and the amount of it is increasing as well. When this occurs, you tend to:

a) Think that negative situations are evolving quicker than you can come up with solutions
b) Think that situations are moving so quickly that you feel overwhelmed
c) Think that there is no time between now and the impending threat
d) Numerous risks and threats seem to all appear at the same time

How Does CBT Address Unhelpful Thinking Styles?

Now that you understand unhelpful thinking styles, including what they are and how they present themselves, we are now going to look at how CBT addresses and improves upon these unhelpful thinking styles.

The benefit of learning what these unhealthy thinking styles are is that an individual would be better able to recognize when those unhealthy thoughts are happening and then use CBT to control them. When a person has a good understanding of these unhelpful thinking styles, they will be able to interrupt it when it is happening and say to themselves, for instance, "I'm catastrophizing again." When a person develops the ability to interrupt their cognitive distortions, they will then change their thought process into more helpful land positive instead. In the next subchapter, we will learn how a person can challenge their unhelpful thinking styles.

By determining whether your negative thoughts are justified or not, a person can control it and manage their depression or anxiety.

Challenging Your Cognitive Distortions

A person can begin to reshape their negative thoughts into something more factual and realistic once they learn how to identify their unhealthy thinking styles. In this section, you will find all the different cognitive distortions categorized. There are specific questions that I have provided for you to ask yourself to start developing different thoughts.

I want to make a note here for you to keep in mind; changing your thoughts is a process that requires a lot of effort, dedication, and awareness. Don't get frustrated if you are not finding success right away as you have probably had these unhealthy thoughts for a long time. It will take some time to make changes, so don't expect this to happen overnight. The more a person simply just pays attention to their thought processes, the easier it becomes.

Probability Overestimation

If you find that you have thoughts about a possible negative outcome, but you are noticing that you often overestimate the probability, try asking yourself the questions below to reevaluate your thoughts.

· Based on my experience, what is the probability that this thought will come true realistically?
· What are the other possible results from this situation? Is the outcome that I am thinking of now the only possible one? Does my feared outcome have the highest possible out of the other outcomes?
· Have I ever experienced this type of situation before? If so, what happened? What have I learned from these past experiences that would be helpful to me now?
· If a friend or loved one is having these thoughts, what would I say to them?

Catastrophizing

· If the prediction that I am afraid of really did come true, how bad would it be?
· If I am feeling embarrassed, how long will this last? How long will other people remember/talk about it? What are all the different things they could be saying? Is it 100% that they will talk about only bad things?
· I am feeling uncomfortable right now, but is this a horrible or unbearable outcome?
· What are the other alternatives for how this situation could turn out?
· If a friend or loved one was having these thoughts, what would I say to them?

Mind Reading

· Is it possible that I know what other people's thoughts are? What are the other things they could be thinking about?
· Do I have any evidence to support my assumptions?
· In the scenario that my assumption is true, what is so bad about it?

Personalization

· What other elements might be playing a role in the situation? Could it be the other person's stress, deadlines, or mood?
· Does somebody always have to be at blame?
· A conversation is never just one person's responsibility.
· Were any of these circumstances out of my control?

Should Statements
· Would I be holding the same standards to a loved one or a friend?
· Are there any exceptions?
· Will someone else do this differently?

All or Nothing Thinking
· Is there a middle ground or a grey area that I am not considering?
· Would I judge a friend or loved one in the same way?
· Was the entire situation 100% negative? Was there any part of the situation that I handled well?
· Is having/showing some anxiety such a horrible thing?

Selective Attention/Memory
· What are the positive elements of the situation? Am I ignoring those?
· Would a different person see this situation differently?
· What strengths do I have? Am I ignoring those?

Negative Core Beliefs
· Do I have any evidence that supports my negative beliefs?
· Is this thought true in every situation?
· Would a loved one or friend agree with my self-belief?

Using this knowledge, the moment you catch yourself exhibiting these unhelpful thinking patterns, begin to ask yourself these questions to start changing your thought process. Keep in mind that the basis of CBT is the theory that a person's thoughts directly influence their emotions and behavior. By simply paying attention to your thoughts and changing them before it spirals, a person should be able to control both their emotions and behavior.

How to Prevent Procrastination

Since procrastination happens mostly due to a person's unhelpful thinking styles, CBT is a great technique to challenge this because it revolves around monitoring one's thoughts. The first step to using CBT to manage your procrastination is simply trying to be more aware of what you're thinking. Due to our fast-paced society built up of thousands of decisions a day, many people go through their daily lives on auto-pilot to minimize the number of decisions they have to make. They do this to preserve their energy as making that many conscious decisions every day is exhausting. If this is your first time practicing CBT, all I am asking you to do is try to be mindful of your thoughts. Find moments of peace and quiet, and just pay attention to what's going on in your mind. Are you letting yourself be in the present moment, or do you think about the hundreds of things you need to get done this week?

Once you have practiced this a little bit, we will begin learning about unhelpful thinking patterns and styles. People who procrastinate often have adopted numerous unhelpful thinking styles, making them feel like certain tasks are extremely daunting. Combining your newly found mindfulness with unhelpful thinking styles, you will soon be able to identify when you are exercising those unhelpful thinking styles.

CHAPTER 5
Examples Of Cbt

In this chapter, we will be discussing a few tips and tricks to help you start making the small changes you need to incorporate CBT in your lifestyle.

Examples of CBT in Action

In this subchapter, we will be focusing on a real-life example of a person using CBT to treat depression using a case study of an adolescent suffering from depression in Puerto Rico. The purpose of this example is to give you an idea and visualization of what actual CBT sessions look like and what types of benefits you can gain from them. Although depression highly varies in every person, and so do treatment methods, this example can give you a general idea of what a formalized CBT structure would look like.

This case study explores the traits associated with using CBT as a treatment and focuses on showcasing the challenges and high variability in CBT and depression. This adolescent has been diagnosed with MDD (major depression disorder) and will be going through 12 standard CBT sessions. This client is 15 years old and showcasing symptoms of highly dysfunctional attitudes, low self-esteem, and high suicidal ideation. The CBT structure used will be the 12 standard sessions of therapy with an additional family intervention. Scientists conducted this trial based on the statistics that people found about 80% effectiveness when using CBT and/or IPT to treat their depressive disorders. They are looking to prove further how CBT can provide significant changes in a person's depressive symptoms. Let's dive into some details of this case study.

The patient of this case study is an adolescent female 15-years-old of age. She is living with her parents and one younger sibling. The parents of this patient have had some significant marital problems and have been discussing divorce and have separated numerous times. Her mother has a history of mental disorders, including depression and anxiety, while her father has been struggling with bipolar disorder (BPD) and is still going through treatment. There is a history of her father being hospitalized numerous different times due to his serious psychiatric symptoms.

The patient has been suffering in external ways, including failing a few classes in school. Her family was attempting to find a new school for her due to her poor academic performance and social struggles. The symptoms that she has been suffering from are; difficulty concentrating, hopelessness, insomnia, irritability, anxiety, low self-esteem, guilt, overeating, crying, and frequent sadness. She also reported that she has difficulties with relationships due to her negative outlook regarding her academics and physical appearance. She also feels a lot of guilt due to her parent's relationship problems. This patient had a medical history of asthma, obesity, and vision problems. Three years ago, she was diagnosed with MDD and treated on and off for about two years using a blended approach using antidepressants and psychotherapy. Her first depressive episode was triggered when her crush at school rejected her. Her latest episode is heavily related to her academic and social abilities at school and her parents' divorce.

In this case study, the patient who needs treatment uses a manual-based CBT, which has proven to have success in adolescents who suffer from depression. The patient became connected to a clinical psychologist for this study whose job is to direct the CBT sessions and report CBT's effects in this adolescent.

During the first four sessions of the patient's CBT, the therapist focused on teaching her about the relationship and influence of a person's thoughts on their mood and behavior. The therapist taught her about strategies that can challenge your unhealthy thought patterns/cognitive distortions to change them into more positive thoughts. The therapist asked the patient to record their mood at the beginning of every session. The therapist used the log of their moods for discussion. The patient also participated in CBT homework assignments, including logging her positive and negative thoughts and identifying her cognitive distortions. During these first four sessions, the patient's mood had high fluctuation. She cried many times during these sessions and expressed feelings of low self-esteem, sadness, and guilt. The main dysfunctional thoughts that she had were mostly about her traits. For instance, she thought of herself as "ugly and stupid" and that "people look at me because I'm fat." She had anxiety about going to a new school and struggling with whether or not she would be able to fit in. She also struggled with guilt regarding her parents' marriage and thought about her fault that her parents are fighting. By the fourth session, the patient began to succeed at challenging her negative thoughts and replacing them with more positive ones such as "I am capable of making new friends" and "I have a good sense of humor and am very artistic." However, many of her negative thoughts were still persistent, and they focused mostly on her parents' relationship. By the end of four sessions, her self-esteem seemed to be improving as she was beginning to share her artistic abilities with her therapist.

The next four sessions were focused around helping the patient increase the amount of time on activities that she found pleasant; her goal setting and time management seemed to improve her overall mood. The homework that she had to do during these sessions included completing a weekly schedule, logging her pleasant activities daily, creating very specific goals, and making a plan to achieve them—the patient's mood significantly improved by the 5th session. The therapist theorizes that it was most likely due to her grades increasing, making new friends, and having an overall better experience at her new school. She was also getting along better with her new teachers. The patient reported that her depression symptoms were decreasing. The positive experiences that she gained at her new school benefitted her during her CBT sessions. The therapist used those positive experiences as a tool to challenge any unhelpful or negative thoughts that the patient had by providing evidence that proved her theories wrong. For instance, she now has evidence that she can cope in a new school and that she was likable. Therefore, she was able to use this evidence to challenge self-deprecating thoughts that she used to have like "People look at me because I'm fat" or "I am ugly and stupid." She also reported that the number of negative thoughts she's been having had decreased significantly, and she found it valuable that her therapist was verbally reinforcing this.

Through these sessions, the patient found out that one of the main challenges for her when it comes to enjoying leisurely activities or social gatherings was her negative thoughts. These negative thoughts included things such as, "Others will reject me" or "I'll make a fool of myself" and worrying about whether or not her parents will give her permission to do her specified pleasant activities. By keeping track of her scheduled pleasant/leisurely activities, the patient began to manage her time better to include chores and homework. Using this documentation, the therapist and patient evaluated together to have a good balance of chores and responsibilities with pleasant activities. She now knows that doing pleasant activities significantly boosted her mood, so she has to make adjustments accordingly. The therapist also participated in role-plays to convince and negotiate permission with her parents when she wanted to participate in social gatherings or leisure activities. Throughout these second set of sessions, the patient's self-esteem improved continuously as she could vocalize these improvements. She began to have more confidence in her appearance and exhibited healthier behaviors like better posture, grooming, and a general increase in confidence. The patient also reported that she was handling stressful situations much better. For instance, when kids at school were teasing her, she now could simply ignore it rather than beginning to have negative thoughts about herself due to what other people were putting into her head. This example shows us that the patient is beginning to grasp the skills learned in CBT, such as techniques to stop negative thoughts to decrease negative emotions.

The last set of sessions with the client (sessions 9 – 12) focused on exploring how her interpersonal relationships affect her mood. The therapist let her know that they will be focusing on increasing her social support, maintaining it, and improving her assertiveness regarding communication. The patient acknowledged that she has a good social network of supportive people but vented about how one of her friends would often put her down, which led to her negative thoughts about her attractiveness and overall abilities. The therapist helped the patient by examining what expectations she had regarding friendships. The patient showed a more passive communication style, which hurt feelings when she did not continuously meet her emotional needs. Therefore, the first two sessions of this last set focused on helping the patient develop her assertiveness level through role-play exercises. Later on, the patient reported that some upsetting incidents had happened at school. Still, she appeared to be handling those situations better by using the strategies she has studied and learned during the first set of sessions.

Throughout the last few sessions, the patient reported that she was still feeling emotions of sadness, guilt, and anger regarding her parents' divorce. She specifically reported that she was uncomfortable by witnessing her parents' communication problems and how they often spoke badly about each other behind each other's backs. She felt that in an attempt for her parents to communicate with one another, she acted as a messenger. She also talked to the therapist about experiencing emotional and physical abuse between her parents through her experience of living through multiple separations over the last decade. The therapist suggested that they could explore the possibility of having a CBT session with her par, to better communicate with the parents how their communication problems are negatively affecting the patient. The patient agreed to this. During the session, the parents and therapist discussed how the parents' behavior harms the patient's depression symptoms and suggested how they should go through marital counseling or therapy. At the end of the session, the parents admitted that they have significant problems and agreed to go to couples therapy in hopes of working things out.

At this point, the patient has completed the standard CBT session at 12 sessions total. However, the patient was still showcasing depression symptoms at a severe level and still met the criteria for MDD. Therefore the therapist decided to give her additional sessions until she no longer met the criteria for MDD. These four additional sessions focused mostly on the patient's feelings around her parents' separation and divorce. The therapist made sure to teach the patient how to manage her feelings about her parents' divorce to lower its impact on her daily functioning and mood.

Throughout the additional sessions, the therapist found out that the main negative thoughts that the patient has were related to being fearful of how her father may leave their family and never speak to her again. She stated that she was scared of her father remarrying into another family with people she might not get along with. These thoughts were challenged in therapy sessions using CBT, where the therapist asked the patient to find evidence of her thoughts becoming a reality. Through this, the client discovered many of her friends who had similar family situations still had healthy relationships with their parents and new relatives, and she remembered the fact that her father had told her that even if he and his wife had separated, that he would still always be there for her. She then realized that things might be more positive if her parents had just separated, and the number of fights decreased. The therapist also continued practicing role-playing with the patient regarding her father's possibility of leaving the marriage and how it would affect her relationship with her father.

Upon the end of her additional sessions, the depressive symptoms were not in the moderate range and not in the severe range. She also no longer met the criteria for MDD, and her self-esteem had significantly improved, and the therapist reported that her suicidal ideation and dysfunctional attitudes had significantly decreased. During the following months, six months later, and one year later, the therapist noted that she maintained her improvements and that her depressive symptoms were not mild compared to severe.

The therapist focused on closure with the patient to reinforce the patient's improvements in her coping skills and mood during the last session. The therapist also taught her relapse prevention strategies as relapse is a part of the recovery process with many mental disorders. The relapse prevention strategies that the therapist taught her included using CBT strategies to manage her mood, recognizing when she needs treatment, and monitoring her depressive symptoms. The therapist also spent time teaching her mother how to monitor her daughter's depressive symptoms properly and emphasized the importance of helping her daughter seek treatment if symptoms worsen over time.

At the end of this case, the researchers found that the use of CBT had appeared to successfully reduce the patient's depressive symptoms, including her suicidal ideation and dysfunctional attitudes. They found that the number of CBT sessions required to achieve results was 16, four more additional sessions from the standard 12 session structure. Additionally, the patient showed improvements continuously over several months, post-treatment regarding her depressive symptoms, low self-esteem, and dysfunctional attitudes.

The most significant stressor that highly affected the patient's symptoms were the marital problems between her parents. While the use of antidepressants and CBT individually seemed to have been effective in this case study, the use of both may have proven to be a more effective alternative option in terms of achieving recovery and preventing relapse. Moreover, booster sessions post-therapy help improve her even further after the end of therapy. Other additional aspects that may have helped would be family therapy between her parents solely and with her included as well.

This case did a great job illustrating some of the challenges that CBT may face when treating depression with many variabilities. Cases like this one who focused on a patient with significant family issues often require additional stressors and some modifications in the CBT manual to address those significant issues, specifically to offer a complete treatment.

Throughout this case, we found evidence that one of the most effective methods for this patient was interrupting her unhelpful thinking styles and finding evidence to prove that her thoughts are incorrect and that she needed to foster a more positive mindset. It seemed that finding evidence herself created the buy-in necessary to continue using her therapist's skills. The client also participated in homework and worksheets related to CBT, which helped her practice skills outside of sessions, which likely contributed to the treatment's overall effectiveness. I hope this case study did a good job explaining how CBT would work in reality and how the client's effort makes a difference in the treatment outcome. Unlike other talking therapies, CBT requires the patient to practice and do homework outside of the sessions to train and apply the skills she has learned in real life. It seemed like CBT alone was sufficient enough to treat her severe depression, but perhaps with the use of antidepressants or other lifestyle changes at the same time would have sped up and increased the effectiveness of her treatment.

Example CBT Sessions

In this stage of the book, you now understand what CBT, anxiety, worry, and unhelpful thinking styles are. We will move on to some real-life examples of CBT being used to treat anxiety and/or depression. These examples are from real therapy sessions where CBT is being used to help the client reshape their thoughts and change their thinking styles. In these examples, the therapist identifies the client's issues and then teaches the client how to use CBT to change their thoughts.

Example #1 (Session One):

Maria is 40 years old and has two children; Vish and Christina, 17 and 13. She has a husband named Jey, he is a lawyer, and Maria works as a designer at an interior design firm. She is in therapy due to her recurring panic attacks and has a history of depression. Here is the transcript below between Maria and her therapist, Putri.

Maria: I haven't been able to function normally due to my recent panic attacks. My heart begins to race, and I feel like I start to suffocate. I just start to focus on; I'm not sure what...

Putri: Try to focus in on it; give me a feeling of what is happening.

Maria: Well, actually, the panic occupies my entire body. I can't think about anything else. My heart beats fast, and my blood feels hot and racing as well. I feel like I'm dying. I've already gone to the ER three times because I thought I was in danger.

Putri: So you feel total preoccupation?

Maria: Jey, my husband, was late, and he had also misplaced the car keys. The whole situation was insanity. After I got everyone together, I began to sob. I was crying so much it was uncontrollable.
Putri: And what happened after that?
Maria: Well, after I got myself together, I started getting ready for work. Once I got into my car, I just froze. My heart began racing again, and I felt tingly all over my arms. I thought I was going to faint. My first reaction was to get myself to the ER, so I phoned Jey, but he was still too upset and angry from the incident that morning. He said that I should call someone else to take me to the ER. So I called my only other option, my son Vish, and he left school to take me to the ER. I felt so embarrassed. Once I got assessed by the doctor, she said that there was nothing wrong with me.
Putri: What are your thoughts on that?
Maria: I was confident that there was something wrong with me. The physical feelings that I felt were so real; you know the tingling and heart-racing feelings? The doctor suggested that a psychiatrist would be able to help me.
Putri: So did you go and make an appointment with the psychiatrist?
Maria: Yes, I went through a series of tests, and all of my results came up as negative. I had another appointment with a different psychiatrist the following day, and he prescribed me some medication that seems to be helping a little bit.
Putri: Do you know what kind of medication your doctor prescribed?
Maria: I think they were antidepressants. I'm not completely sure.
Putri: Have you ever been depressed before?
Maria: Yes, think so. I feel like I have battled with bouts of depression throughout my whole life.
Putri: Give me some examples of your battles with depression.
Maria: Well, for example, I feel like I'm battling it presently. My husband is a lawyer, which means that he is pretty much busy all day every day. Vish is a teenager and is also always busy. Christina is becoming an adolescent and at the stage where she feels like her mother is always wrong. I feel like I'm walking on eggshells all the time. I constantly feel like I am worthless. I feel like all hope is lost.
Putri: So you feel like everything is bleak and that there's no hope?
Maria: Yes, it feels like my life is miserable. Almost like a tragedy.
Putri: So it's not just right now?
Maria: No.
Putri: Tell me more about what you are feeling.
Maria: Well, when I was 13, the same age as Christina, that was when my mom passed away from cancer. It felt like my whole life came to an end. I loved my mother so deeply, and I constantly think about what things would be like for my daughter if I --
Putri: If what happened to your mother happened to you?

Maria: Yes.
Putri: What would it be --?
Maria: I wonder about what it would be like for my daughter.
Putri: And you were the same age?
Maria: Yes, I was 13 when my mother passed. Same as Christina's age now. I always think back to all the things I had to do during that time. I was the oldest sibling, so I took care of my dad, sister, and brother.
Putri: What was it like? What did you have to do?
Maria: My father became depressed and turned to drink; I had to care for him. I would be the first to get up out of everyone to get breakfast ready for them. I had to make sure that my father went to work, which meant that I had to wake him up. After that, I would have to make everybody's lunch and then get myself ready for school. I would have to check on my siblings throughout the day as well.
Putri: How do you feel about this?
Maria: Not dealing with our feelings was a constant theme in my family. We just pushed our feelings down and away.
Putri: Pushed them down? I see. What was going on with your dad? You mentioned he was depressed and drinking a lot.
Maria: Yeah. He missed my mom a lot, and I understood, I missed her too. I was the eldest kid, so he took out a lot of things on me.
Putri: How did he take things out on you?
Maria: He would constantly joke about how I was too dumb to go to college. I wanted to go to college.
Putri: So he would criticize you?
Maria: Yes, he constantly belittled me, and I would tell him that he was belittling me. He would get upset then say that he was only kidding.
Putri: How did you feel about this?
Maria: It made me feel awful because you can't get that angry over a 'joke.' I was confused. I took all those feelings and stuffed them as far down as possible.
Putri: Is stuffing down feelings something that you still do now?
Maria: Yes, Jey has that tendency to criticize as well.
Putri: And when you face that kind of criticism, how does it make you feel?
Maria: I get really angry, and afterward, someone usually tells me that it was only a joke.
Putri: What do you do when you get those feelings of anger?
Maria: I stuff the feelings down. I don't like to deal with those feelings.
Putri: If you are stuffing your feelings down the way you do with Jey and your father, how is it impacting you? What price are you paying to stuff your feelings down?
Maria: I don't know.
Putri: I'm not sure either. This could be a possible topic that we can discuss in our future sessions.

Maria: Yes.

Putri: Alright, let's see if I'm on the same page as everything you've told me so far. Please let me know if I'm wrong. You are dealing with many waves of panic, and you've experienced it through the attacks you've been having. These attacks even led you to the ER a few times. It seems like you are going through a few different things.

Maria: Yes, correct.

Putri: Let's start by discussing what we can do about these panic attacks. Then, let's talk about your business of stuffing down feelings and its impact on you.

Putri: I would like you to start noticing when you begin having panic attacks and the exact moment you begin to push down your feelings. We will discuss that in our next session.

In this example, the therapist Putri was able to identify two important issues. The first was Maria's panic attacks; we will continue to explore this in more detail and design a treatment plan since this is impacting her life largely. Once Maria has the skills to keep her panic attacks under control, we can address the next issue: the impact of her depression and anxiety.

Example #2 (Session Two):

Putri: Let's get a better feel regarding your panic attacks. Tell me about the worst incident you've had.

Maria: It was a crazy morning; everybody had just left. Jey left for work, and the kids went to school. Once everyone left, I just started uncontrollably crying. Somehow, my crying ended, and I began getting ready for work.

Putri: Let's try something here. Could I ask you to please close your eyes and sit back on your chair?

Maria: Yes, sure.

Putri: (During this time, Putri explores Maria's thought process and feelings related to the incident. She used an imaging technique to guide her into noticing the thoughts she normally wouldn't pay attention to. This exercise aims to help Maria see that her thoughts and emotions are connected and how it influences her physical behavior, like her panic attacks.)

Maria: I got into my car as I was about to leave for work. Suddenly, I felt lightheaded. I got scared because I thought the panic attack was happening again. My heart began to beat very quickly, and I started to breathe heavily and very fast. I thought I had to go to the ER because I had a heart attack. I was scared that I wouldn't make it to work. I thought that I had to get help. I felt like my lungs were closing in on me.

Putri: (Putri identifies that Maria is having a catastrophic appraisal of the situation by her describing that she thinks she is dying again and is having a heart attack. Putri wants to make Maria understand that she is

not a passive victim during her panic attacks. If she were able to look at her situation from a new perspective, she would have the ability to cope differently. She can change her outcome)
Putri: In this situation, everybody had left for school or work, and you felt a sense of relief. Then you had those feelings of panic?
(For Putri to help Maria see the connection between triggering stimulus, thoughts, emotions, and behavior, Putri decides to use the metaphor of a visual clock to help Maria see her situation. Noon is the situation, 3:00 are her apprehensive feelings, anxiety, and fear, 6:00 is the catastrophizing thoughts that happen automatically, and 9:00 is the behaviors of a panic attack.)
Putri: So the thoughts you were having: "Is this happening again? I'm losing control!" Then, being unable to get to work and looking for help, "Who can I call to help me?" It sounds like it is a cycle.
Maria: Yes, a vicious cycle.
Putri: That is something we can look into. (With Maria's agreement, Putri helped her explore ways that Maria can begin to monitor her thoughts)
Putri: One action that you will need to start doing is to note down when you begin to have anxiety feelings. Be very specific when this happens. Then, we will be able to keep a record of the specific anxiety-inducing situations.
Maria: Yes.
Putri: (The focus of treatment here will be to bring Maria's panic attacks under control. Putri will do this by teaching Maria how anticipatory fear plays a role like panic attacks. Putri will also help Maria with the following; managing her symptoms, paying attention to warning signs, interrupting her inner critic, breathing exercises, relaxation training, cognitive restructuring (to help control catastrophic thinking styles), interpreting anxiety symptoms accurately, and learning coping techniques.
At the end of session two, Putri has decided that she will implement the following cognitive behavioral therapy treatment plan for Maria:
- Learning about the role that anticipatory fear plays in panic attacks
- The nature of panic disorders
- Skills to help manage anxiety/panic symptoms
- Cognitive restructuring (changing unhelpful thinking styles)
- Graduated exposure to panic stimulus
- Coping technique practices

Example #3 (Session Three):

Maria: So, last Tuesday when I went into Christina's room in the evening to let her know dinner was ready, she started screaming at me about --
Putri: (Continues to monitor Maria's anxiety by focusing her attention on Maria's thoughts and feelings during the situation)

Putri: Help me get a better understanding of what happened with Christina. How did you feel after you walked into her room?
Maria: Well, I felt like the blow-up wasn't my fault. I felt that it was unfair. I felt I couldn't have done anything about it. I began to think that in this family, nothing I do is right.
Putri: What happened next?
Maria: I left her room. I was able to see how I'm starting to get riled up about it. I felt that my chest was starting to close in on these feelings.
Putri: (Putri notices that Maria tends to interpret her feelings of irritation and anger, as tenseness and anxiety. She describes them in physical terms such as a tight feeling in her chest.)
Maria: My whole body felt very tense, but I tried to calm myself down.
Putri: Did you feel the sensation of your heart racing again?
Maria: Yes, my heart was racing, and I felt suffocated.
Putri: What happened this time?
Maria: I just left the situation by leaving Christina's room.
Putri: (After doing a quick review of the remainder of Maria's thoughts, feelings, emotions, and behaviors, Putri decided to focus on Maria's hyperventilation issue. She wants to help Maria regulate her bodily changes during hyperventilation and give Maria a sense of control. Putri decides to use a method called diaphragmatic breathing as a coping tool for Maria.)
Putri: When humans experience panic attacks, one thing that tends to happen is that they begin to breathe very quickly. That is the act of hyperventilation. When people experience this type of breathing pattern, it tends to make their body tenser. Many of the feelings you are having during your panic attacks; tingling, dizziness, hot and cold flashes, are all symptoms related to how you are breathing. Therefore, if you learn to control your breathing, this could help you stop the vicious cycle of hyperventilation. Let's take a minute to practice breathing exercises.
Maria: Sure.
Putri: Great. This exercise will give you an idea of what you can control. Please sit back in your chair in a comfortable position. Then, close your eyes.
Putri: Start by taking a slow and deep breath, filling your chest, and hold it. Slowly breathe out and pretend that you are trying to cool down a spoonful of soup by breathing on it but not spilling it. Feel the warmth and calmness of the soup. Think about the things we talked about regarding how being tense contributes heavily to the vicious cycle of hyperventilation.
Putri: (In the next step, Putri decides to focus on Maria's panic disorder's cognitive component. Putri decides to examine Maria's thoughts using an anecdote.)
Putri: Another part of this vicious cycle that we've been talking about are the kind of thoughts that you are having. For us to both get a better

understanding of them, let's go back to the situation with Christina and examine what you thought and how you felt at each stage.
Maria: Alright.
Putri: Let's pick up at the moment where you had gone into Christina's room. What did she say?
Maria: She began yelling at me about always invading her privacy. I thought this was so unfair. I didn't do anything wrong by telling her dinner was ready.
Putri: So, she was attacking you at random?
Maria: Yes, I didn't do anything. After I left her room, I thought to myself how I can never do the right things for my family and how I am always wrong. I can never be right, and I'm worthless.
Putri: So these thoughts of "I never do anything right, and I am never appreciated" are those a part of your vicious cycle?
Maria: Yes, exactly.
Putri: I'd like to look into two components of this. The first is, what are the things you can do to alter your thoughts? The second is, where are these thoughts and feelings coming from? Let's begin with trying to break out of that cycle, and then we will move onto figuring out where your feelings are coming from.
Maria: Okay.
Putri: Walk me through what those thoughts were.
Maria: So, I thought her yelling at me wasn't fair. It's not like I did anything wrong. All I did was to let her know dinner was ready. When I began to leave her room, I started thinking that this is the way it always is. I am always in the wrong, and I don't do anything right. I'm a complete failure.
Putri: (When Maria describes these thoughts, Putri identifies them as automatic thoughts. She will help Maria find the evidence that supports or doesn't support her thoughts to help Maria see things from a different perspective)
Putri: Is it true that you are a complete failure?
Maria: No, absolutely not.
Putri: Exactly, you are not a complete failure.
Maria: No, I am not.
Putri: In what ways are you not a complete failure? (Putri is challenging Maria to find evidence to prove that she is not always failing.)
Maria: I've done so much in the past, and I had to raise my siblings when I was still a child. My dad kept telling me that I wouldn't be able to go to school because I was too dumb. I made sure that I went to school anyway and paid for it entirely myself.
Putri: So you paid your way through school?
Maria: Yes.
Putri: So when your mom died, you had to take care of your dad and your siblings.

Maria: Yes.
Putri: Then you went to school?
Maria: Yes. My dad was extremely depressed, and all he did was drink. He kept telling me that I was too dumb to study interior design. To prove him wrong, I got into an art school and studied it.
Putri: So you were still able to do it despite the things he said about you?
Maria: Yes.
Putri: Do you have any other examples of why you are not a failure?
Maria: Well, Vish got into a good college and is about to go, so that's awesome. The kids are pretty good.
Putri: How about your work? Do you feel like you are failing there as well?
Maria: Not at all; I've been working there for over two years already.
Putri: So, based on your assumption that you are a complete failure, does that fit the description of someone who accomplished all those things?
Maria: No, I guess not.
Putri: (The discussion of supporting evidence which is consistent with the fact that Maria is not a failure, has given her hope. She began to cry softly at this realization)
Putri: Do the assumption of you being worthless and a complete failure match with the evidence of who Maria is?
Maria: No.
Putri: (To validate Maria's reactions, Putri decides to help Maria appreciate how the feelings she had are not only normal but appropriate given her childhood and the history with her dad)
Putri: The tears that I see you have right now are a sign of how much you are in touch with your feelings.
Maria: Yeah, they are.

In the next three sessions with Maria and Putri, they used various CBT techniques to help Maria develop control over her panic attacks. They used diaphragmatic breathing to manage her hyperventilation and anticipatory fear. They identified Maria's cognitive distortions and her tendency to catastrophize and practice fact-checking her thoughts to determine what is true and what is just a thought. Putri encouraged Maria to practice those coping skills every day as a form of an experiment to see what worked with her and what didn't.

To analyze the last three examples, we were able to see how the therapist identified areas where Putri was displaying unhelpful thinking styles. In this case, she was catastrophizing. We were able to see how the therapist uses CBT to identify these thoughts, some of which are automatic, and help the client find their evidence inconsistent with those thoughts. The breathing techniques help soothe anxiety symptoms and help you refocus your attention from the anxious thoughts to simply managing your physical symptoms. You may have noticed in the above examples that the client and therapist must be working as a team. There needs to be full cooperation and dedication to practicing new skills, thought processes, and coping techniques. CBT is only effective if the client is practicing it throughout their daily life.

CHAPTER 6
Preventing Relapses With Cbt

Many people that are on their journey of recovery worry about losing the progress that they've made by having an anxiety relapse. A previously suffering person but has their symptoms reduced wants to make sure that they keep these positive changes as long term as possible. This desire is very understandable, as slipping back into old habits will cause a loss of improvement. Luckily, there are many methods and ways to prevent relapses and control lapses.

The first thing we should learn about is the difference between a lapse and a relapse. We define a lapse as a brief return to old and unhealthy habits. It is very common and normal and often happens from fatigue, low mood, or stress. We define relapse as a complete return to old ways of thinking and behaving during anxiety bouts. Individuals who have a relapse tend to be doing all the same things they used to be doing before learning new managing anxiety methods. Keep in mind that although lapses can lead to relapses, they don't necessarily have to. You have the power to stop a lapse from turning into a relapse.

Here are some examples showcasing a lapse compared to a relapse:

Let's say that you had a phobia of riding in a car. If you have been going through CBT, you have probably learned that it is not the best idea to avoid riding in a car. Instead, you have been taught to practice breathing exercises, practice coping thoughts, and gradually work your way up to riding in a car.

So if one day you were out with a group of coworkers and one of them offered to drive the group to dinner, and you avoided the situation by making an excuse and walked home instead, this would be called a lapse.

If you entirely went back to your old and unhealthy routines such as being late to work due to you avoiding to ride in a car or missing social events because they are too far to walk to, this would be called a relapse.

So when does a lapse turn into a relapse? Usually, the things you say to yourself after having a lapse can lead you to get back on track or lead you into a relapse. If you perceive your lapse as a sign of failure, you may likely give up and have a relapse. However, if you perceive your lapse as a slip-up or a mistake that you could recover from, then you likely will not have a relapse.

If we went back to our car, phobia example:

If you ended up avoiding riding in a car with your coworkers by making an excuse and walked home, but at the end of the day, you said: "I fell into my old habits again, I better start practicing some CBT techniques this week to get myself back on track."

This event would result in your lapse ending, and you continue to face your fears and healthily manage your anxieties.

However, if you ended up avoiding the car situation with your coworker and at the end of your day, you said, "All the hard work I put into managing my anxiety around cars was a complete waste! I am now right back where I started because I'm such an idiot. I guess there is no cure, after all, might as well stop trying."

This situation would result in your lapse turning into a relapse. It will likely cause you to stop practicing CBT any further, and you will return to your old and unhealthy habits.

Although relapses are common when it comes to recovering from anxiety, there are a few causes that could play a role in a relapse:

- Stressful life events that happen to you during or after recovery can cause a relapse. These events can include things like relationship changes, family conflict, and grief.
- Stopping early in treatment is another way for a relapse to happen. Since anxiety isn't a quick fix, you need to stick with your treatment plan for months after you start feeling better to reduce the risk of relapse. Failure to do this may cause you to slip back into old habits.
- A feeling of inability to cope using your prescribed anxiety management strategies is a common cause of relapse. If you feel like the strategies you were taught and given aren't working, seek help from your therapist or counselor to figure out a new strategy to get on track. Most people have to experiment with different strategies to find one that works best for them.
- Changes in your lifestyle or physical health also play a huge role in relapses. If you have physical illnesses like heart disease or diabetes, it could increase your risk of worsening anxiety. Big lifestyle changes can also create lots of stress, which prevents you from taking the time to practice managing your anxiety.

How to Prevent Relapses

The best way to recover from a relapse is to prevent one in the first place. By taking all prevention measures and being prepared, you are at a much lower risk of relapse than someone unprepared. Keep in mind that it is normal to have lapses and relapses, but your mindset dictates whether you get back on track or stay in a state of relapse. Below are a few tips on preventing lapses and relapses:

- **Practice, practice, and practice!** The best way to prevent a relapse is to frequently practice your CBT knowledge and skills or whatever treatment plan you learned. If you are always practicing, you will be in a good position to handle whatever life throws in your ways. You can fit in practice by making a schedule for yourself, consisting of which skills you will practice every week. This practice may include breathing exercises or

challenging unhelpful thinking styles. Get friends or family to hold you accountable for practice.
- **Know your red flags!** People are less likely to have a lapse or relapse when they know when they are most vulnerable in having one. For instance, most lapses and relapses happen during times of stress or big change.
-
    - Make a list of warning signs that indicate when your anxiety is increasing. This list can include:
        - Increased feelings of anxiety
        - Increased responsibilities at work, home, or school
        - Increased anxious thoughts
        - Arguments with family/friends
        - Major life changes (e.g., death, childbirth, wedding, moving)
        - Avoidance of activities (e.g., social events, exercise, going outside)
    - Make a plan on what to do when you encounter your danger signs in terms of coping. This plan includes:
        - Practice CBT more frequently.
        - Taking some time-outs for yourself to practice things like breathing exercises or mindfulness
        - Relaxing (hanging out with friends, reading a book, watching a movie)
- **Coming up with new challenges!** Just like everyone around you, you are a work in progress. There are always different ways and strategies that you could use to improve yourself to make life more fulfilling and enjoyable. A good technique to prevent relapses is to challenge yourself to work harder on further anxiety. You can start by making a list of situations that are anxiety-inducing and begin to work on them. People are less likely to fall back into old habits if they continue to challenge themselves by learning new and different ways to manage their anxiety.
- **Learn from your lapses!** Keep in mind that it is normal to have lapses occasionally. At times of greater stress, people are more vulnerable to a lapse if they are still learning to cope with anxiety. The good thing about this is that you can learn a lot about yourself from these lapses. You can use your lapses as an opportunity to figure out what the situation was that led to a lapse. Knowing that situations make coping more difficult for you can help you prepare for the next time. You can create a plan to help you cope with more difficult future situations.
    - Was it due to you having anxious and upsetting thoughts?

- Was your anxiety very high at the time?
- Were you doing something different?
- Did you know that the situation would be difficult, or was it a surprise to you?
- **Knowing the facts!** In this chapter, you have learned that what you are thinking after a lapse largely affects your chances of a full relapse. If you think you are a failure, you are more likely to give up and fall into a relapse. Consider these things:
    - It is not possible to entirely fall back into 'square one.' You cannot unlearn all the techniques or skills taught to you through treatment (e.g., CBT). Being at square one means experiencing anxiety but having no knowledge of how to deal with it. Since you have started your treatment and have learned many skills during it, you know how to handle anxiety, and therefore, you are not back to 'square one.'
    - People who relapse can 100% get back on track. Even if it had taken you months to practice ways to manage your anxiety symptoms, it wouldn't take you just as long to get back to where you were before the relapse. Once you get back to practicing your anxiety management skills, you'll be on your way to mastering it again in no time.
- **Be kind to yourself.** Keep in mind that lapses and relapses are normal and part of the process. Don't punish yourself harshly during moments of weakness as it doesn't help you in any way. Instead, it is more useful to understand that people make mistakes sometimes. If you don't speak to someone else like that, you should not be speaking to yourself like that. It may be very helpful to have a lapse to understand your weaknesses and learn where to focus your practice.
- **Reward yourself!** Ensure you are taking the time to reward yourself for the hard work to manage your anxiety. To encourage motivation, give yourself a treat now and then. Rewards can range from buying yourself something nice, going out for a nice meal, or just taking some time to pamper and relax. Learning to manage anxiety is hard work, so make sure you are celebrating all your progress.
- **Exercise:** Researchers have found that regularly exercising can be just as effective as medication when treating depression and anxiety. Exercises cause an increase in the 'feel-good' brain chemicals in the brain, such as serotonin and endorphins. These chemicals also trigger the growth of new brain cells and connections similar to what antidepressants do. The best part about exercise is that you don't need to do it intensely to benefit. Even a simple 30-minute walk can make a huge difference in a

person's brain activity. For the best results, people should aim to do 30 – 60 minutes of aerobic activity every day or on most days.

Social Support: Like I mentioned earlier, having a strong social network reduces isolation, which is a huge risk factor in depression and anxiety. Make an effort to keep in regular contact with family and friends (ideally daily) and consider joining a support group or class. You can also opt to do some volunteering to get the social support you need while helping others.

- **Nutrition:** The ability to eat healthily is imperative for everyone's mental and physical health. By eating small meals that are well-balanced throughout the day, you can minimize your mood swings and keep energy levels up. Although you may crave sugary foods due to the quick boost of energy that it can bring, complex carbohydrates are much more nutritious. Instead, complex carbohydrates can provide you with an energy boost without a crash at the end.
- **Sleep:** A person's sleep cycle has strong effects on mood. When a person does not get enough sleep, their symptoms of depression or anxiety may get worse. Sleep deprivation causes other negative symptoms like sadness, fatigue, moodiness, and irritability. Not many people can function well with less than seven hours of sleep per night. A healthy adult should be aiming for 7 – 9 hours of sleep every night.
- **Stress reduction:** When a person is suffering from a lot of stress, it intensifies their depression or anxiety and increases their risk of developing more serious depression or anxiety disorders. Try to make changes in your life that can help you reduce or manage stress. Identify which aspects of your life creates the most stress, such as unhealthy relationships or work overload, and find ways to minimize their impact and the stress it brings.
- **Practicing Gratitude:** An important method of overcoming depression and/or anxiety is to practice gratitude frequently. When you are in a moment of stress, anxiety, or depression, take some time to think about all the things in your life that you appreciate. The things you can think about include all the worldly things that you have like your home, your computer that you use all the time, or even just your favorite type of coffee that you have at home. Practicing gratitude also includes expressing gratitude towards your positive qualities. For instance, being grateful for your strength, your intelligence, and any other good qualities that you know you have. This method is very simple and gives people a better perspective on their lives. People are often stuck in the moment of distress and can't take a step back to see the bigger picture. Removing yourself from the distress in a moment and

thinking about all the things you are grateful for makes a huge difference in changing your mindset. Remember to be kind to yourself, even in the darkest moment.

Recognize the Mind-Body Connection: You may be wondering how these two seemingly unrelated things (the inner world and the outer body) can be considered related. In this section, we will look at how the mind and body connect and cannot be disconnected. To illustrate this, we will look at an example that involves food and eating.

Over time, your body learns that eating certain foods (like those containing processed sugars or salts such as fast food and quick pastries) makes the body feel rewarded, lively, and happy for some time after you eat these foods. When you feel sad or worried, your body senses this and looks for ways to remedy these negative feelings. Your brain then connects the mind's emotions with the reward that it knows that it can get from eating certain foods. As a result, it decides that eating these foods will turn their inner state from negative to positive and make it feel better. As a result of this process that happens in the background without you being aware of it, you consciously feel a craving for those foods (like sugary snacks or salty fast-food meals), and you may not even be aware of why you are craving them. This process all happens in a brief second in the subconscious mind. If you decide to give in to this craving and eat something like a microwave pizza snack, your body will feel rewarded and happy for a brief period. This act reinforces the concept believed by your brain that craving food to make itself feel better emotionally has worked.

If you feel down and guilty that you ate something that was unhealthy, your brain will again try and remedy these negative emotions by craving food. This example shows how a cycle of emotional eating can begin without being any the wiser.

Because scientists and psychiatrists have come to understand this process in the brain and the body, they know that the mind and body are inextricably connected. Food craving and even being overweight can often indicate emotional deficiencies or emotional struggles. For this reason, it is essential to address the underlying issues when trying to deal with depression or anxiety. By dealing with the root causes of the problem, you can prevent it from recurring. If you try to break free of anxiety for some time without looking deep within to find the causes of the struggles you are having, the chances of falling back into your old state are very high. Therefore, it is necessary to address the root causes to end your struggles once and for all.

This is another great way that we can come to understand issues like depression and anxiety, as they manifest themselves in the physical body. If you find yourself experiencing food cravings, take a look deep within and find out the underlying issues.

Like I mentioned earlier, the best way to get back on track from a relapse is to simply not have one. However, relapses and lapses are normal throughout a person's recovery journey, so if you find yourself having a lapse or a relapse, get some help. This strategy could be in talking to a therapist, a friend, or a family member. The quicker you seek help, the easier it will be to come back from that relapse. Remember, every little bit of progress is still progress, and that is not all entirely lost due to a relapse. You still have a plethora of knowledge and skills that you've gained throughout treatment, and you can once again put those skills to use.

Although Cognitive Behavioral Therapy is the most effective type of speaking therapy out there, it is important to try other treatment plans to further your recovery. More important than trying out different types of treatment is refusing to give up. Many treatments aren't quick-fix solutions; they require you to do exercises, practice, and apply them in real life. Continuing to exercise skills and techniques you have learned to overcome anxiety and depression is the main pillar. Even if you have recovered from your mental disorders and have gone months, even years, without incident - it is still important to set aside some time to practice the techniques that worked for you. This time is important to prevent lapses that could lead to a full relapse. By continuing to practice skills that have worked for you, you will be well-equipped to deal with a potential lapse if something traumatic or sudden change happens to your life. Preparation is key.

CONCLUSION

For all the knowledge you have learned for this book to work, you must be consistent with practicing CBT. Most people don't see the effects of CBT visibly until 4 – 5 weeks in, sticking with it and not giving up is something you need to pay attention to. Always start slow and get the fundamentals down. Start by simply just paying more attention to your thoughts, and you will slowly be able to see the patterns of your negative thinking. The moment you can realize this, you can begin to interrupt your negative thinking. The hardest part of the whole CBT process is to change your mind from being on autopilot to paying attention to thoughts. That act of doing that is tiring, so some people do not find success with CBT when they don't practice. However, the mind and brain are a very malleable function in the body; the brain can adapt to whatever is healthiest and best for your body. By practicing and actively paying attention to your thoughts, your habits will begin to change, and you'll slowly start to see the error of your thinking styles.

I want you to pat yourself on the back for taking the initiative to learn more about how to treat mental disorders. This learning is not an easy task. When a person is suffering from the symptoms of common conditions like anxiety or depression, it's hard for them to think clearly and strategically. The fact that you found the motivation to purchase and read this book and finish it and a considerable achievement. You learned in-depth about cognitive behavioral therapy and how it treats anxiety and depression. This information about CBT is one of the most important takeaways as CBT can provide people with the right tools to combat their negative thoughts.

So what's next beyond this book? Well, if you think you have a mental disorder, please ask for help. This help doesn't have to be in the form of a therapist, but just talking to friends and family can offer you the guidance you need to take your next step. If you are thinking of getting a therapist, reach out to multiple, and get a consultation. Make sure that the therapist you choose has experience treating specific things that you are feeling. Do also make sure that you and this therapist get along, and you are comfortable with how they are approaching your treatment. Keep in mind that most therapies require you to practice outside of the sessions. Be prepared to take the extra time so you can practice everything you learned from therapy.

I hope this book helped you learn everything you need to know regarding cognitive behavioral therapy and mental disorders. As someone who has experienced this for many years, I have one thing to say to you. Don't be so hard on yourself, and it will get better for you. Taking the first step in finding help will start a chain effect in overcoming your mental disorders. Everything will become easier once you equip yourself with the right tools to handle any situation that life throws at you. Don't give up.

DESCRIPTION

Have you ever wondered how you can find solace and peace from anxiety and depression? Have you ever wondered how you can break free from negativity and follow your dreams? Have you ever wondered if there is more out there for you? Are you feeling stuck and are struggling to get out of your slump? Are you someone that feels like their mental disorders always burden them? Have you been looking for a solution and a way out? This book will provide you with this and so much more!

CBT has shown significant results for up to 75% of people who use it as treatment. The effectiveness level rises to 90% if combined with other methods.

This book will teach you how to apply CBT to your mental health care, and it will also teach you other methods that help treat mental disorders. By combining CBT with other treatments like meditation and lifestyle improvements, the entire treatment set's effectiveness rises significantly. Upon opening this book, you can expect to find the following information;

- What cognitive behavioral therapy is
- The history behind Cognitive Behavioral Therapy
- The modern-day uses of CBT
- How CBT works
- Different types of CBT techniques
- Benefits and drawbacks of CBT
- How to start small with CBT
- Anxiety disorders, causes, and symptoms
- Depression disorders, causes, and symptoms
- The science behind depressive disorders
- Different types of depression
- The benefits and drawbacks of choosing CBT as treatment
- How to use CBT to manage your anxiety and/or depression
- Other methods that also help to manage anxiety and/or depression
- How to prevent relapses
- Effects of untreated depression, anxiety, and other mental disorders
- Where to turn for assistance after reading this book
- Real-World Examples of CBT sessions

This book will explore the theories and functions of Cognitive Behavioral Therapy and how it works to treat disorders like Anxiety and Depression. We will start this book by learning more about how CBT works when used and how it compares to other therapy types. We will then learn about what anxiety is, its symptoms, and different types. With all of this information and more, you will be well-equipped to begin taking control of your life.

When a person is suffering from psychological distress, the way they perceive certain situations can become contorted, this could cause negative behaviors. By learning about CBT and how it can help you, you can begin to change these thoughts and start seeing things.

The mind and the brain are very malleable and are always ready and willing to change. The brain can adapt to whatever is healthiest and best for your body. By practicing and actively paying attention to your thoughts, your habits will begin to change, and you'll slowly start to see the error of your thinking styles.

Overall, this book aims to teach you how to use CBT; its purpose is to educate you on all topics related, so you understand why CBT uses the strategy that it does. Understanding that, people are more likely to stay committed to the process than give up if they don't see results right away.

www.ingramcontent.com/pod-product-compliance
Lightning Source LLC
Chambersburg PA
CBHW071509070526
44578CB00001B/485